OCCASIONAL PAPER 204

# Monetary Union in West Africa (ECOWAS)

Is It Desirable and How Could It Be Achieved?

Paul Masson and Catherine Pattillo

INTERNATIONAL MONETARY FUND
Washington DC
2001

© 2001 International Monetary Fund

Production: IMF Graphics Section
Typesetting & Figures: Choon Lee

**Cataloging-in-Publication Data**

Masson, Paul R.
  Monetary union in West Africa (ECOWAS) : is it desirable and how could it be achieved? / Paul Masson, Catherine Pattillo. — Washington, D.C. : International Monetary Fund, 2001.
     p.   cm. — (Occasional paper, ISSN 0251-6365 ; no. 204)

  Includes bibliographical references.
  ISBN 1-58906-014-8

  1. Economic Community of West African States. — 2. Union economique et monetaire Ouest africaine. — 3. Monetary unions — Africa, West.  4. Africa, West — Economic integration.  5. Monetary policy — Africa, West.  I. Pattillo, Catherine A. (Catherine Anne).
II. International Monetary Fund.   III. Occasional paper (International Monetary Fund) ; no. 204.

HC1000.M27 2001

Price: US$20.00
(US$17.50 to full-time faculty members and
students at universities and colleges)

Please send orders to:
International Monetary Fund, Publication Services
700 19th Street, N.W., Washington, D.C. 20431, U.S.A.
Tel.: (202) 623-7430     Telefax: (202) 623-7201
E-mail: publications@imf.org
Internet: http://www.imf.org

recycled paper

# Contents

| | Page |
|---|---|
| **Preface** | v |
| **I Introduction** | 1 |
| **II The Proposed Monetary Union** | 4 |
| **III Historical Experience and the Current Situation in West Africa** | 8 |
| WAEMU | 8 |
| Other Countries in West Africa | 9 |
| Performance of WAEMU and Non-WAEMU ECOWAS Countries | 10 |
| Assessment | 10 |
| **IV What Is a Monetary Union?** | 14 |
| **V Lessons from the Experience of Currency Unions** | 16 |
| **VI The Benefits and Costs of a Common Currency for West Africa** | 19 |
| Benefits of a Fixed Exchange Rate Relationship | 19 |
| Conditions for Monetary Stability of the Currency Union | 22 |
| Can a Common Currency Stimulate Other Forms of Integration? | 25 |
| **VII Options for Implementing Monetary Union in West Africa** | 26 |
| The "Second Monetary Union" | 26 |
| The Second Stage: Full Monetary Union in ECOWAS | 29 |
| **VIII Conclusions: The Perspective of Regional Integration** | 30 |
| **Appendices** | |
| I Economic Policies in Non-WAEMU Countries | 32 |
| II Existing and Failed Currency Unions | 36 |
| III Comparative Performance of the CFA Franc Zone | 40 |
| **References** | 42 |
| **Tables** | |
| 2.1. ECOWAS Members: Basic Indicators | 4 |
| 2.2. ECOWAS: Position of Non-WAEMU Members vis-à-vis the Convergence Criteria | 5 |
| 2.3. WAEMU: Position of Members vis-à-vis the WAEMU Convergence Criteria | 6 |

## CONTENTS

    3.1. ECOWAS: Selected Indicators    10
    3.2. ECOWAS Members: Exchange Arrangements    12
    5.1. Characteristics of Monetary Unions    17
    6.1. ECOWAS: Patterns of Trade    20
    6.2. ECOWAS Members: Correlation of Changes in Terms of Trade    22
    6.3. ECOWAS Members: Production Structure    23

**Figures**

    2.1. Membership of the CFA Franc Zone and ECOWAS    5
    3.1. WAEMU versus Non-WAEMU Countries: Selected Indicators    11
    6.1. ECOWAS Members: Terms of Trade    21

---

The following symbols have been used throughout this paper:

... to indicate that data are not available;

n.a. to indicate not applicable;

— to indicate that the figure is zero or less than half the final digit shown, or that the item does not exist;

– between years or months (i.e., 1997–98 or January–June) to indicate the years or months covered, including the beginning and ending years or months;

/ between years or months (i.e., 1997/98) to indicate a crop or fiscal (financial) year.

"Billion" means a thousand million; "trillion" means a thousand billion.

Minor discrepancies between constituent figures and totals are due to rounding.

The term "country," as used in this paper, does not in all cases refer to a territorial entity that is a state as understood by international law and practice; the term also covers some territorial entities that are not states, but for which statistical data are maintained and provided internationally on a separate and independent basis.

# Preface

The authors are especially grateful to Christian François and Ernesto Hernández-Catá for encouraging them to undertake this study, for valuable suggestions, and for obtaining the support of the African Department, and to Ousmane Doré for supplying data and participating in discussions with officials. The authors are grateful as well to a number of their colleagues at the IMF and the World Bank, in particular Trevor Alleyne, David Andrews, Luis de Azcarate, Girma Begashaw, Eduardo Borensztein, Vincent Caupin, Dominique Guillaume, Anne-Marie Gulde, Elliott Harris, Hiroyuki Hino, Charles Humphreys, Robin Kibuka, Alexander Kyei, Célestin Monga, Gonzalo Pastor, Mark Plant, Papa Ousmane Sakho, Jesús Seade, Reinold van Til, Luisa Zanforlin, and Alessandro Zanello. The authors also would like to thank Agnès Bénassy-Quéré, Daniel Cohen, Max Corden, Patrick Guillaumont, Sylviane Guillaumont-Jeanneney, Charles Soludo, and George Tavlas for comments and discussion; Grace Juhn, Manzoor Gill, and Jungyong Shin for research assistance; Jacqueline Irving for excellent editorial and substantive input; and Celia Burns for typing the manuscript.

This paper has also benefited from discussions with officials in Abuja, Accra, Brussels, Dakar, and Paris. In particular, valuable suggestions and comments were received at the ECOWAS Secretariat, the European Commission, the BCEAO, and at central banks and government ministries in France, Ghana, and Nigeria. The views expressed here are those of the authors, however, and do not represent the official views of those institutions or of the International Monetary Fund.

# I Introduction

On April 20, 2000, in Accra, Ghana, the leaders of six West African countries[1] declared their intention to proceed to monetary union among the non-CFA[2] franc countries of the region by January 2003, as a first step toward a wider monetary union including all the ECOWAS[3] countries in 2004. The six countries committed themselves to reducing central bank financing of budget deficits to 10 percent of the previous year's government revenue; reducing budget deficits to 4 percent of GDP by 2003; creating a Convergence Council to help coordinate macroeconomic policies; and setting up a common central bank. Their declaration states that, "Member States recognize the need for strong political commitment and undertake to pursue all such national policies as would facilitate the regional monetary integration process."

The goal of a monetary union in ECOWAS has long been an objective of the organization, going back to its formation in 1975, and is intended to accompany a broader integration process that would include enhanced regional trade and common institutions. In the colonial period, currency boards linked sets of countries in the region. On independence, however, these currency boards were dissolved, with the exception of the CFA franc zone, which included the francophone countries of the region.[4] Although there have been attempts to advance the agenda of ECOWAS monetary cooperation, political problems and other economic priorities in several of the region's countries have to date inhibited progress. Although some problems remain, the recent initiative has been bolstered by the election in 1999 of a democratic government and a leader who is committed to regional integration in Nigeria, the largest economy of the region, raising hopes that the long-delayed project can be revived.

The plan to create a second monetary union (in addition to that constituted by the West African Economic and Monetary Union, or WAEMU),[5] as well as a full ECOWAS monetary union, raises a number of questions about the advantages and disadvantages of various alternative arrangements and strategies. There is clearly an important political dimension behind the recent initiative, but it is nevertheless important to carefully examine the economic benefits and costs. The institutional design of the non-WAEMU monetary union could take a number of different forms, including the creation of a new currency or the adoption of an existing one, the formation of a single central bank or its coexistence with national central banks, and a peg (e.g., to the euro or a currency basket) or a flexible exchange rate for the external exchange rate policy of the common currency. The second stage, involving the merger of the two currency unions, raises some of the same issues. The second stage also raises additional issues, such as whether the French Treasury's guarantee of convertibility of the CFA franc to the euro, at a fixed parity, would continue.

The purpose of this paper is to evaluate whether a monetary union makes economic sense, to discuss the institutional requirements for a successful monetary union, and to consider how best the political

---

[1]The meeting was attended by three heads of state, Presidents Olusegun Obasanjo of Nigeria, Jerry Rawlings of Ghana, and Lansana Conté of Guinea, as well as representatives from Liberia, Sierra Leone, and The Gambia. Cape Verde, the remaining non-CFA ECOWAS member, has a currency peg to the euro with the support of Portugal, and was not a signatory of the "Accra Declaration on a Second Monetary Zone." Mauritania, a founding ECOWAS member, recently withdrew from the regional organization.

[2]CFA stands for "Communauté financière africaine" when it refers to the West African franc zone.

[3]ECOWAS, or Economic Community of West African States, is composed of the seven countries mentioned in the first footnote, plus the eight countries that are members of the West African Economic and Monetary Union—namely, Benin, Burkina Faso, Côte d'Ivoire, Guinea-Bissau, Mali, Niger, Senegal, and Togo.

[4]Guinea and Mali left the CFA zone upon independence, but Mali later rejoined.

[5]WAEMU is an eight-member economic and monetary union. The French acronym for WAEMU is UEMOA (l'Union Economique et Monétaire Ouest Africaine). The common currency of the WAEMU countries, the franc de la Communauté financière de l'Afrique (CFA franc), is issued by a single central bank, the Banque Centrale des Etats de l'Afrique de l'Ouest (BCEAO). WAEMU's CFA franc is pegged to the French franc, which since 1999 has been a subunit of the common European currency (euro).

# I INTRODUCTION

momentum for a union can be channeled toward a fundamental improvement in underlying policies. After giving details of the ECOWAS monetary union project, the paper reviews the economic situation of the ECOWAS members, with the objective of evaluating the ease with which they can proceed to a common currency. Next, the paper considers the requirements for creating a successful monetary union, drawing lessons from existing monetary unions. Naturally enough, the performance of the CFA franc zones—one of which, WAEMU, is comprised of eight countries in West Africa—provides some of the most relevant lessons. Although the CFA franc has delivered low inflation, growth performance in WAEMU has not been consistently better than in other sub-Saharan African countries, and trade among member countries remains relatively low. The exchange rate and banking crisis in the second half of the 1980s and early 1990s showed that fiscal policy must be disciplined and central banks must be insulated from indirect financing of budget deficits through the banking system. Other currency unions, in particular the European Union's 12-member Economic and Monetary Union, illustrate the need for extensive institutional preparation and the need for participants first to achieve economic convergence.

In considering the possible net economic benefits of monetary union, similarity of production structures, factor mobility, flexibility of wages and prices, and symmetry of shocks hitting the economies all enhance the attractiveness of such a union. In fact, there are major differences among the West African economies. In particular, Nigeria, a major oil exporter, faces a very different pattern of terms of trade shocks than the other economies of the region. Moreover, existing internal trade among the region's countries is quite low, although there is undoubtedly considerable informal trade that is not recorded. Of course, one of the reasons for proceeding to monetary union quickly is to promote improvement in macroeconomic policies and to enhance prospects for other aspects of regional integration, including regional trade. The empirical literature is not definitive, but it does suggest some boost to the trade among members of a monetary union.

Next, the paper discusses various institutional options for implementing monetary cooperation within ECOWAS. A distinction is made between full monetary union and looser forms of monetary cooperation, such as an informal monetary union. The attractiveness of the two options depends in part on the *purposes* of monetary union. On the one hand, if the union's main purpose is to bring about exchange rate and macroeconomic stability, it may be preferable for the participants to institute mutual surveillance and keep exchange rates within (perhaps very narrow) fluctuation bands or opt for a common external peg. These looser forms of monetary cooperation could achieve this goal at a lower cost than would a full monetary union and its institutional requirements. On the other hand, a full monetary union may have advantages over looser forms of cooperation, such as providing a more effective "agency of restraint" (Collier, 1991) for domestic policies. In this context, national central banks acting alone may not be able to achieve the necessary discipline, but a supranational institution might be able to do so, through peer pressure and externally imposed sanctions. Setting up a central bank and eliminating national currencies will take longer than the planned timetable, however, and it would be wasteful of resources to create new institutions if they disappear shortly thereafter, when the second monetary union merges with WAEMU.

Several strategic decisions must be made if the full monetary union option is selected initially or, in any case, at the time of the creation of a full ECOWAS monetary union. The first choice is that of a central bank for the monetary union. Unfortunately, none of the non-WAEMU countries has a central bank with a track record of currency stability and low inflation. Nigeria, which accounts for more than half the population of ECOWAS and 75 percent of the GDP of the six countries proposing an initial monetary union, would be a natural candidate to form the nucleus of monetary union, but Nigeria has a history of high inflation and the Nigerian currency is inconvertible. A second choice associated with a full monetary union is whether the region's common currency(ies) should have an external exchange rate anchor, such as a peg to the euro. An independent peg of each of the currencies to the euro would provide exchange rate stability within the region (as well as with the 12-member euro area and with the neighboring six-member Central African CFA zone). A euro peg thus could deliver some of the advantages of a common currency without extensive institutional preparation. Choosing to peg to a basket rather than to a single currency, however, would permit some insulation from the fluctuations among major currencies. Finally, the issue of whether the French Treasury's guarantee of convertibility[6] will continue would arise if and when

---

[6]The French Treasury currently has sole responsibility for guaranteeing convertibility of CFA francs into euros, without any monetary policy implication for the Bank of France (French central bank) or the European Central Bank. The two CFA central banks maintain an overdraft facility with the French Treasury, subject to operating rules that have applied since 1973. Each CFA central bank must keep at least 65 percent of its foreign assets in its operations account with the French Treasury; provide for foreign exchange cover of at least 20 percent for its sight liabilities; and impose a cap on credit extended to each member country equivalent to 20 percent of that country's public revenue in the preceding year.

a merger of the second monetary zone and WAEMU is contemplated.

This paper discusses these issues and considers the proposal for a monetary union from a wider perspective of the prospects for regional integration. The paper concludes that it is important to recognize that monetary union is neither necessary nor sufficient to achieve other aspects of regional integration, in particular intraregional trade, as the contrasting examples of the North American Free Trade Agreement (NAFTA) and the CFA zone illustrate. Moreover, the objective of monetary union should not be allowed to distract attention from addressing the serious domestic problems faced by countries in the region, which will mainly be resolved by "putting one's house in order" and opening up the economies externally by removing the obstacles to trade posed by tariffs, other forms of protection, poor transportation infrastructure, and divergent regulations and codes. Instead, the process of strengthening mutual surveillance should be used to provide a powerful channel for each country to converge on good policies, and this could be the most important major benefit from regional integration. Thus, instead of trying to meet a very short deadline for monetary union, the countries of the region should invest their energies in reinforcing convergence on low inflation, sustainable fiscal policies, and structural policies necessary for strong growth. A degree of exchange rate stability as well as the benefits of mutual surveillance over macroeconomic policies could be achieved through a looser form of regional monetary cooperation.

# II   The Proposed Monetary Union

Recent plans for monetary union come as a response to a political commitment by ECOWAS heads of state, who met on December 9–10, 1999, in Lomé, Togo, to accelerate the pace of regional integration.[7] In particular, the Accra Declaration on a Second Monetary Zone, signed on April 20, 2000, by six non-WAEMU West African countries, expressed their intention to establish a second common currency in the region by 2003 and to work toward a single currency for ECOWAS by 2004. National ministers of finance, trade and commerce, foreign affairs, and integration, together with national central bank governors, sit on an ECOWAS Convergence Council, empowered to oversee implementation of the process. A Technical Committee is tasked with working out the structure and regulatory framework for a regional central bank, and other preparatory activities. The Council recently approved the Technical Committee's recommendation to establish the West African Monetary Institute in early 2001 to serve as a transitional institution to a future, common central bank.

Table 2.1 presents some basic statistics for the countries in the region. There is a wide range of income levels and country sizes, with Nigeria constituting by far the largest country in the region, but also one of the poorest. All of the countries face serious challenges to reduce poverty, improve health care, and invest in education. Figure 2.1 shows the overlapping membership of the CFA franc zone and ECOWAS; only one of the two regional economic and monetary groupings using the CFA franc, WAEMU, is part of ECOWAS.

The Accra summit established convergence criteria, which the signatories committed themselves to achieve by end-2003:

---

[7]The impetus for monetary union also seems to have been stimulated by the formation of the euro zone. See Irving (1999).

**Table 2.1. ECOWAS Members: Basic Indicators**

| Country | GNP Per Capita in U.S. Dollars, 1998 | Population in Millions, mid-1998 | Life Expectancy at Birth in Years, 1997 | Percent of Population Living on Less Than US$1 a day | Primary School Enrollment Ratio, 1995–96 |
|---|---|---|---|---|---|
| Benin | 388 | 6.0 | 53 | 45 | 78 |
| Burkina Faso | 260 | 10.7 | 44 | 66 | 40 |
| Cape Verde | 1,127 | 0.4 | 68 | ... | ... |
| Côte d'Ivoire | 754 | 14.5 | 47 | 35 | 71 |
| Gambia, The | 347 | 1.2 | 53 | ... | 77 |
| Ghana | 399 | 18.5 | 60 | 45 | ... |
| Guinea | 576 | 7.1 | 46 | 40 | 48 |
| Guinea-Bissau | 161 | 1.2 | 44 | ... | ... |
| Liberia | ... | 3.0 | 47 | ... | ... |
| Mali | 263 | 10.6 | 50 | 70 | 45 |
| Niger | 204 | 10.1 | 47 | 75 | 29 |
| Nigeria | 228 | 121.3 | 54 | 60 | ... |
| Senegal | 570 | 9.0 | 52 | 40 | 68 |
| Sierra Leone | 146 | 4.9 | 37 | ... | ... |
| Togo | 327 | 4.5 | 49 | 66 | ... |

Source: World Bank, *African Development Indicators*, 2000.

# The Proposed Monetary Union

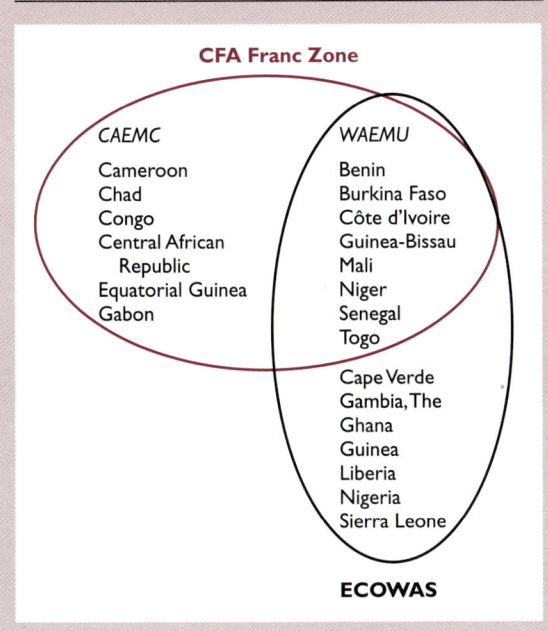

Figure 2.1. Membership of the CFA Franc Zone and ECOWAS

- gross official reserves covering at least six months of imports of goods and services;
- central bank financing of the budget deficit limited to 10 percent of the previous year's tax revenues.

These criteria are the most important ones, although there also are some secondary criteria. Table 2.2 shows the current situation with respect to the criteria for the ECOWAS countries that are candidates to form the "second monetary union."

The WAEMU members have carried out mutual surveillance of policies at the national level for a number of years, and they have recently revised their convergence criteria (see IMF, 2000). Although there has been an attempt to harmonize the ECOWAS convergence criteria with those of the WAEMU,[8] differences remain. WAEMU targets a basic budget balance[9] of at least 0 percent of GDP and an annual average inflation rate of 3 percent, as well as some additional criteria. As shown in Table 2.3, WAEMU countries are generally much closer to reaching their targets than are the non-WAEMU ECOWAS countries; undoubtedly, this is largely because regional cooperation and surveillance among WAEMU countries have a longer history.

- maximum budget deficits, excluding grants, of 4 percent of GDP;
- a rate of inflation of no more than 5 percent;

[8] See Kouyaté (2000).
[9] Defined as total revenue, excluding grants, minus total expenditure, excluding development projects directly financed by external resources, generally on concessional terms.

Table 2.2. ECOWAS: Position of Non-WAEMU Members vis-à-vis the Convergence Criteria[1]

|  | Inflation Rate (Percent) | Gross Official Reserves (In months of imports) | Central Bank Advances (As percent of tax revenue) | Overall Fiscal Deficit[2] (As percent of GDP) |
|---|---|---|---|---|
| Position at end-1999 |  |  |  |  |
| Gambia, The | 1.7 | 5.7 | 32.0 | 4.8 |
| Ghana | 13.8 | 1.5 | 8.2 | 8.2 |
| Guinea | 4.6 | 2.6 | 29.6 | 5.1 |
| Liberia | 4.0 | 0.0 | 0.0 | 0.4 |
| Nigeria[3] | 6.6 | 4.5 | 55.0 | 7.7 |
| Sierra Leone | 34.1 | 2.0 | 70.9 | 14.9 |
| Convergence criteria for end-2000 | <10 | >3 | ... | <5 |
| Convergence criteria for end-2003 | <5 | >6 | <10 | <4 |

Source: IMF staff estimates.
[1] Cape Verde was not a signatory of the Accra Declaration on a Second Monetary Zone.
[2] Excluding grants.
[3] Central bank advances are as a percent of total government revenue.

## II THE PROPOSED MONETARY UNION

**Table 2.3. WAEMU: Position of Members vis-à-vis the WAEMU Convergence Criteria[1]**

|  | Key Primary Criterion | Other Primary Criteria[3] | | Secondary Criteria | | | |
| --- | --- | --- | --- | --- | --- | --- | --- |
|  | Basic fiscal balance[2] (As percent of GDP) | Inflation (Percent) | External public debt (As percent of GDP) | Wage bill[4] (Percent) | Investment financed by domestic resources[4] | Revenue ratio (As percent of GDP) | External current account[5] (As percent of GDP) |
| Position at end-1999 | | | | | | | |
| WAEMU | −1.6 | 0.6 | 129.0 | 36.5 | 16.1 | 15.1 | −8.2 |
| Benin | 0.5 | 0.3 | 59.3 | 33.0 | 11.3 | 13.7 | −10.7 |
| Burkina Faso | −0.6 | −1.1 | 70.5 | 37.1 | 19.3 | 14.0 | −16.3 |
| Côte d'Ivoire | −1.7 | 1.6 | 118.8 | 33.4 | 15.9 | 17.0 | −5.2 |
| Guinea-Bissau | −7.2 | −0.9 | 364.4 | 66.3 | 43.5 | 7.6 | −13.9 |
| Mali | 0.1 | −1.1 | 116.8 | 27.7 | 22.2 | 14.1 | −10.7 |
| Niger | −3.8 | 2.9 | 92.2 | 60.2 | 3.6 | 7.7 | −8.3 |
| Senegal | 2.0 | 0.8 | 94.0 | 34.0 | 21.7 | 16.6 | −7.3 |
| Togo | −1.7 | −0.1 | 116.0 | 51.0 | 2.5 | 13.3 | −10.3 |
| Convergence criteria at end-2002 | ≥0 | ≤3 | ≤70 | ≤35 | ≥20 | ≥17 | ≥−5 |

Source: IMF staff estimates.
[1]Official reserves of member countries are pooled at the regional central bank (BCEAO) and stood at 103 percent of base money at end-1999, equivalent to six months' worth of regional imports.
[2]Defined as total revenue (excluding grants) minus total expenditure excluding foreign-financed investment.
[3]Two other primary criteria concern the change in the stock of domestic and external arrears, which must be negative or nil.
[4]As a percent of tax revenue.
[5]Excluding grants.

The Committee of ECOWAS Central Bank Governors met in Dakar, Senegal, on May 4–5, 2000, to consider the modalities of the ultimate merging of the two monetary unions.[10] They agreed that to ensure the viability of any future single currency for the region, macroeconomic convergence should be achieved first. They noted that in addition to the ECOWAS convergence criteria mentioned above, exchange rate stability against the West African Unit of Account[11] should be achieved. Moreover, the central bank governors set forth three phases intended to lead to monetary union among all the ECOWAS countries:

- *Phase 1.* Harmonizing exchange controls; liberalizing capital markets; establishing rigorous macroeconomic management and reinforcing structural policies; meeting convergence criteria and harmonizing statistics; putting in place a regional single market; liberalizing labor markets; establishing an exchange rate mechanism in which all member countries' currencies would participate; making widespread the use of the West African Unit of Account and revitalizing the West African Clearing House; and creating a Community Monetary Institution, as a transition institution to a single regional central bank.
- *Phase 2.* Evaluating and adapting the policies implemented in Phase 1; reducing the fluctuation margins of the exchange rate mechanism; and harmonizing taxation, in particular on income from saving.
- *Phase 3.* Irrevocably fixing parities and passage to a single currency managed by the single regional central bank.

Although the project has been described in some detail, it is not clear how the list of planned policy measures can be reconciled with the timetable of a monetary union of the non-WAEMU countries (the "second monetary union") by 2003 and overall monetary union by 2004. It also is not clear how the convergence criteria are to be applied—in particular, whether failing to meet them (and by what margin) would preclude participating in either the second monetary union or the full monetary union. The evident intention of Ghana and Nigeria to proceed, although they are both quite far from achieving the

---
[10]Final Communiqué, Eleventh Extraordinary Session of the Committee of Governors of the Central Banks of the Member States of the Economic Community of West African States (ECOWAS), Dakar, May 4–5, 2000.

[11]The West African Unit of Account (WAUA) is linked one-for-one to the special drawing right (SDR). At the May 2000 meeting, central bank governors endorsed the WAUA as the numeraire for evaluating exchange rate stability. Use of the WAUA has largely been restricted to accounting purposes within the ECOWAS bureaucracy.

convergence criteria, raises questions about the role of the convergence criteria.

Finally, details are lacking on how the two transitions—one toward the "second monetary union" and the other toward the full regional monetary union—are to fit together. For example, it is not clear how a newly created single central bank for the non-WAEMU countries would be merged with WAEMU's longstanding central bank, the Banque Central des Etats de l'Afrique de l'Ouest. Moreover, the time horizons for this aspect of the two transitions seem unrealistic, with establishment of the non-WAEMU central bank now planned for end-2002 followed by some merger of the two institutions by 2004. A decision to maintain both banks would be wasteful, in terms of both human and financial resources.

# III  Historical Experience and the Current Situation in West Africa

By virtue of their membership in the CFA zone, the ECOWAS countries that are part of WAEMU have followed a very different path from the non-WAEMU countries. After a brief overview of macroeconomic performance of the WAEMU group, this section will consider the following issues. Could a West African monetary union potentially serve as a vehicle for broader regional integration and could it promote improved domestic policies by locking in mutually agreed policy commitments through peer pressure? How well has WAEMU done in this regard? Next, to understand what the non-WAEMU countries could potentially gain or lose from giving up large areas of policy flexibility by forming a monetary union, it is useful to review how well they have used that policy flexibility. What has been the history of policy regime choices, particularly exchange rate and trade policy, in each of the non-WAEMU countries, and how have these choices affected macroeconomic performance?

## WAEMU

Aiming to build on the cooperation in the monetary sphere established though the long-standing West African Monetary Union, the member countries, Benin, Burkina Faso, Côte d'Ivoire, Mali, Niger, Senegal, and Togo, formed the West African Economic and Monetary Union (WAEMU) in January 1994.[12] With the addition of Guinea-Bissau in 1997, this group has been working to foster broader economic cooperation through creation of a single market. The countries in WAEMU have a common, stable, convertible currency—the CFA franc—which has been pegged to the French franc since 1948 and to the euro since 1999. Inflation has been consistently low, although output growth has been subject to large swings.

During the 1986–93 period, the WAEMU countries suffered a severe recession, associated with a prolonged terms of trade deterioration and steep increases in labor costs, which, together with the nominal appreciation of the French franc against the U.S. dollar, led to a substantial real exchange rate overvaluation. These developments were exacerbated by mounting internal imbalances, evidenced by rapidly declining national savings rates. Exports and economic activity weakened, collapsing fiscal balances as both trade and corporate tax revenues fell with the recession. Transfers to public enterprises rose and public sector financing requirements grew, crowding out private investment. Countries began to accumulate domestic and external payment arrears and public debt grew. By 1990–93, real GDP per capita was declining on average 3 percent per year (Hernández-Catá and others, 1998).

As part of the strategy to address these problems, the CFA franc was devalued from 50 CFA francs per French franc to 100 CFA francs in January 1994. Following the devaluation, exports turned around, led by increases in volumes of traditional exports. Improved profitability in the tradable sectors contributed to a strong growth performance: 5 percent real GDP growth translating into 2 percent growth in real GDP per capita during 1994–98. Following a surge in prices associated with the devaluation, inflation declined rapidly to under 4 percent by 1998. During 1994–98, output, exports, and investment increased more rapidly than in other sub-Saharan African countries.

In recent years, WAEMU countries have taken steps toward greater regional integration and coordination of macroeconomic policies by adopting convergence criteria, establishing a common external tariff, harmonizing taxes, and establishing structural funds to further a more balanced development across the union. There are, however, questions about how effectively trade liberalization and the common external tariff have been implemented. Evidence suggests that private interest groups have pushed to have many locally produced goods moved into tariff categories with the highest protection (World Bank, 2000). Non-tariff barriers such as road blocks and administrative harassment still hamper intra-zone trade.

---
[12]At present the WAEMU treaty coexists with the WAMU treaty but is expected to replace it eventually.

In addition, despite substantial reforms in recent years, the depth of financial markets remains relatively low, and the WAEMU countries still face imposing structural problems in the banking and financial sectors. Although there has been some improvement in compliance with prudential norms set by the regional banking commission, there is still ample scope for further strengthening supervision of the financial system. At the root of the problem is the low level of competition, the weakness of the judiciary system's enforcement of contracts, and the extensive government involvement and management of banks. These structural problems and a lack of creditworthy projects have contributed to excess liquidity in many WAEMU banks since the CFA franc devaluation in 1994. Ideally, the interbank market should help smooth imbalances in liquidity in different countries but, in reality, the interbank market is inefficient and not many banks participate. Given the small size of the financial markets, the development of more diversified financial instruments could occur most naturally at the regional level.[13]

Recognizing that a certain threshold of macroeconomic performance is a prerequisite for moving to a common market, in 1993 WAEMU countries set up five indicators to monitor progress toward macroeconomic convergence. Compliance with the criteria was broadly satisfactory through end-1998 at the WAEMU level, but performance was uneven across the member countries. The system's effectiveness was limited by the lack of sanctions, the absence of a consultation process among members, as well as by poorly designed indicators that were not the most directly relevant to the sustainability of fiscal policy. In December 1999, a new Convergence, Stability, Growth, and Solidarity Pact was adopted, which designated 2000–02 as a convergence phase and 2003 onward as a stability phase. The pact emphasizes one key criterion: the basic fiscal balance must be in equilibrium or surplus. The other primary criteria are convergence to an inflation rate of no more than 3 percent; ratios of domestic and foreign debt to GDP of less than 70 percent; and the nonaccumulation of domestic and external payment arrears.[14] The pact now includes a penalty mechanism, which can include withdrawal of access to the West African Development Bank and suspension of central bank financing, initiated primarily if a country does not comply with the key deficit criterion. Currently, with the exception of Niger, Guinea-Bissau, and Togo, the countries are on track to meet these criteria by 2002 (IMF, 2000).

## Other Countries in West Africa

In the 1970s and 1980s, the policy regimes of many of the non-WAEMU countries in the region were characterized by large government deficits financed by money creation, which led to high inflation (detailed descriptions of country experiences are given in Appendix I). In combination with fixed nominal exchange rates that had parities that were not adjusted, real exchange rates became increasingly overvalued. Excessive domestic credit creation also spilled over into high import demand. The countries reacted to balance of payments difficulties by tightening exchange and trade restrictions, leading to large parallel market premiums for foreign exchange. At some point, the authorities began to lose control and a vicious circle of money-financed deficits and foreign exchange controls led to increases in smuggled or misinvoiced goods, resulting in declining trade tax revenues that further worsened the deficit. The experiences of Ghana, Sierra Leone, and The Gambia are particularly well characterized by this description.

During the mid-1980s and 1990s, a central element of these countries' economic reform programs was the liberalization of exchange and trade restrictions and the movement toward market-determined exchange rates. These reforms have met with variable success. Nigeria's liberalization has been full of starts and stops; highly variable inflation and real exchange rate changes have been associated with terms of trade shocks and long periods of economic mismanagement. Ghana experienced success in restoring incentives for tradable production and improved growth, but losses of fiscal control and poor management of external shocks have created problems in controlling inflation. Appreciation of the real effective exchange rate from 1996 until end-1999 reduced competitiveness. The Gambia and Guinea also had successful stabilizations in the late 1980s and early 1990s that significantly lowered inflation, but were later compromised by political and associated fiscal problems and poor management of shocks. In the 1980s, Cape Verde managed good growth with relatively prudent policies, although the public sector was too large and interventionist. In the 1990s, fiscal laxity slowed progress in Cape Verde; currently, there appears less room for slip-

---

[13]There are signs of recent progress in this area. For example, the Bourse Régionale des Valeurs Mobilières, the regional stock exchange for the WAEMU countries, reportedly is working with the West African Development Bank to introduce new types of bond instruments to attract more small, local investors.

[14]Secondary criteria are that the public sector wage bill should not exceed 35 percent of revenues, investment financed by domestic resources should be at least 20 percent, government revenue should be at least 17 percent of GDP, and the external current account deficit (excluding grants) should be no more than 5 percent of GDP.

# III  HISTORICAL EXPERIENCE AND THE CURRENT SITUATION IN WEST AFRICA

**Table 3.1. ECOWAS: Selected Indicators**

|  | 1975–79 | 1980–85 | 1986–89 | 1990–93 | 1994–98 |
|---|---|---|---|---|---|
| **WAEMU Region[1]** | (Percent) | | | | |
| Real GDP Growth | 5.9 | 1.2 | 2.8 | 0.4 | 5.0 |
| Real GDP Per Capita Growth | 2.8 | –1.9 | –0.2 | –2.7 | 1.9 |
| Export Volume Growth | 6.7 | –2.7 | 3.9 | 2.2 | 7.3 |
| Import Volume Growth | 9.6 | –4.2 | 0.5 | 0.7 | 6.2 |
| Inflation | 14.8 | 7.4 | 1.9 | 0.4 | 10.6 |
|  | (Percent of GDP) | | | | |
| General Government Fiscal Position[2] | ... | –5.5 | –6.1 | –6.7 | –2.4 |
| Gross National Savings | 17.0 | 10.7 | 6.7 | 5.7 | 12.9 |
| Gross Fixed Capital Formation | 18.6 | 15.9 | 13.9 | 13.0 | 16.4 |
| **Non-WAEMU Region[3]** | (Percent) | | | | |
| Real GDP Growth | 0.3 | 0.6 | 3.3 | 4.3 | 3.0 |
| Real GDP Per Capita Growth | –2.4 | –2.4 | 0.5 | 1.4 | 0.0 |
| Export Volume Growth | 6.7 | –2.2 | 7.5 | 4.5 | 6.8 |
| Import Volume Growth | 23.5 | –0.7 | –5.1 | 8.9 | 5.2 |
| Inflation | 29.2 | 31.0 | 28.2 | 27.2 | 30.4 |
|  | (Percent of GDP) | | | | |
| General Government Fiscal Position[2] | ... | –1.7 | –0.7 | –0.2 | –3.5 |
| Gross National Savings | 48.5 | 11.6 | 13.3 | 17.7 | 16.6 |
| Gross Fixed Capital Formation | 20.5 | 15.6 | 18.2 | 19.7 | 18.4 |

Sources: IMF African Department; IMF *World Economic Outlook* databases.
[1]Includes Benin, Burkina Faso, Côte d'Ivoire, Mali, Niger, Senegal, and Togo.
[2]Including grants.
[3]Includes Cape Verde, The Gambia, Ghana, Guinea, Guinea-Bissau, Liberia, Nigeria, and Sierra Leone.

pages given the peg to the euro through the Portuguese escudo. Despite attempts at reform, Liberia and Sierra Leone have experienced poor macroeconomic performance during much of the 1990s due to the economic devastation caused by civil conflicts.

## Performance of WAEMU and Non-WAEMU ECOWAS Countries

The general picture emerging from a comparison of WAEMU and non-WAEMU ECOWAS countries during various subperiods is generally similar to that resulting from comparing CFA countries with the rest of sub-Saharan Africa. Essentially, WAEMU countries have experienced substantially lower rates of inflation than the non-WAEMU countries, but the record with respect to economic activity is mixed. While in 1975–79, growth in WAEMU countries was considerably higher than in neighboring countries of the region, during 1986–93 the WAEMU countries experienced lower real GDP growth, lower export growth, and lower savings and investment. In the 1994–98 period following the devaluation of the CFA franc, however, the WAEMU countries once again had higher GDP and export growth than non-WAEMU countries. Savings and investment ratios rose in the WAEMU countries, while they stagnated in non-WAEMU countries[15] (see Table 3.1 and Figure 3.1).

## Assessment

Most of the non-WAEMU countries have moved away from a system that allocated foreign exchange through non-market processes, contributing to a highly overvalued real effective exchange rate and a very high parallel market premium. These regimes were harmful to growth (Easterly and Levine, 1997; Collier and Gunning, 1999). Trade and exchange rate systems have been liberalized, so that in most countries there are few restrictions on foreign ex-

---
[15]Data for WAEMU here exclude Guinea-Bissau, since it did not join until 1997.

# Assessment

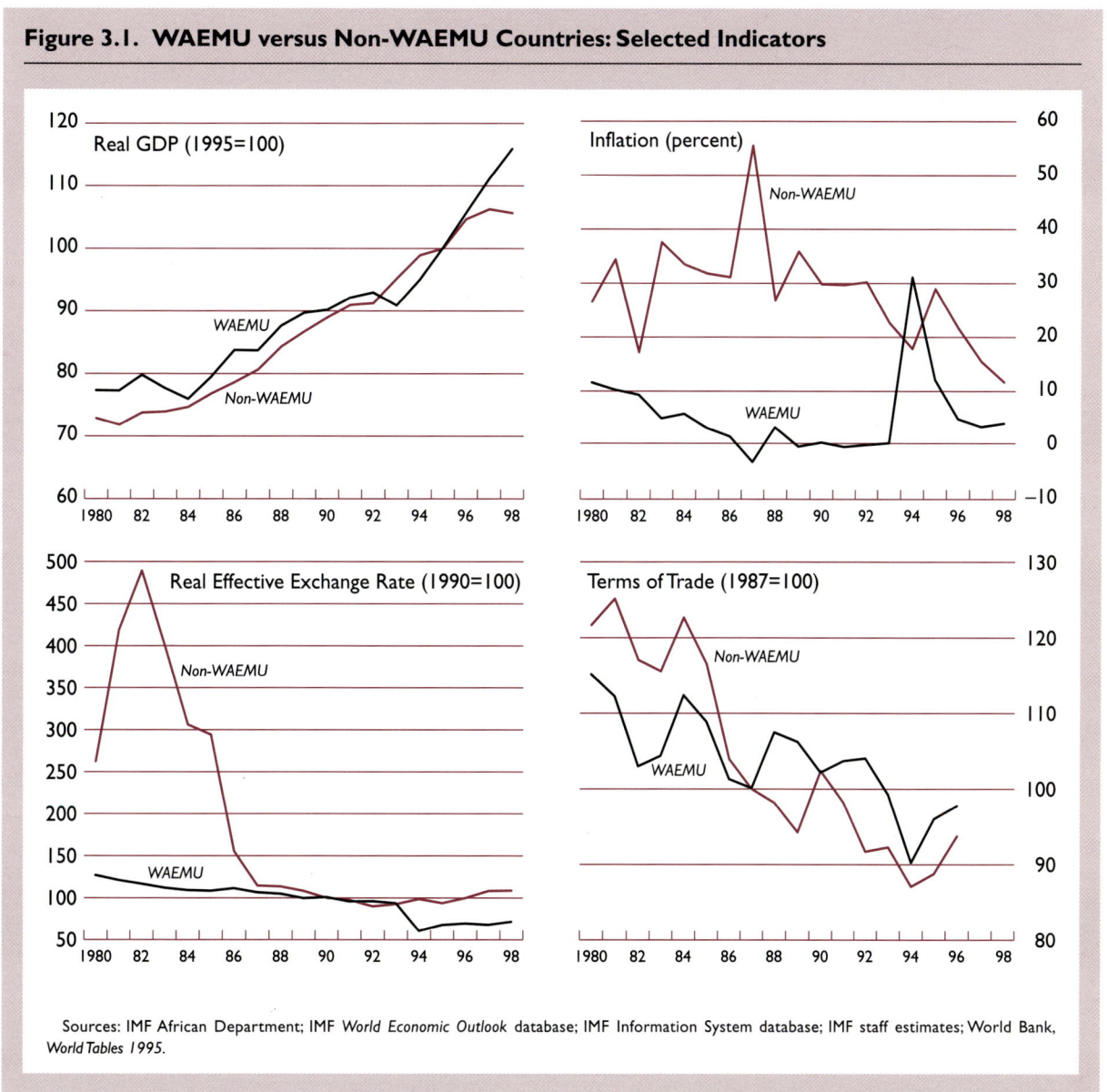

Figure 3.1. WAEMU versus Non-WAEMU Countries: Selected Indicators

Sources: IMF African Department; IMF *World Economic Outlook* database; IMF Information System database; IMF staff estimates; World Bank, *World Tables 1995*.

change for current account transactions. (Table 3.2 gives details of exchange regimes and dates when countries accepted the current account convertibility associated with Article VIII status under the IMF's Articles of Agreement.) Movement toward more market-determined, flexible exchange rate systems has been a centerpiece of reform programs in many of these countries. What do the above descriptions of these countries' policies and performance tell us about the experience under market-determined rates?

- Movements to market-determined rates in the contexts of floats, auctions, and inter-bank markets that made significant progress in unifying official and parallel rates did not lead to immediate, large increases in the level of inflation, as had been feared.[16]

---

[16]Pinto (1991) formalized this expectation, by showing that when the government is a net purchaser of foreign exchange from the private sector, official overvaluation constitutes a large implicit tax on the exportable sector, and unification of the official and parallel market will lead to higher steady state inflation as the government substitutes a higher inflation tax for the lost implicit revenues. Morris (1995), however, showed that when the public sector has a net inflow of foreign exchange, for any given level of government spending, exchange rate unification reduces recourse to central bank financing, hence lowering domestic money creation and inflation.

# III HISTORICAL EXPERIENCE AND THE CURRENT SITUATION IN WEST AFRICA

**Table 3.2. ECOWAS Members: Exchange Arrangements**

| Country | Currency | Exchange Regime | Current Account Convertibility? | Year of Acceptance of Article VIII |
|---|---|---|---|---|
| **WAEMU** | | | | |
| Benin | CFA franc | Peg to euro | Yes | 1996 |
| Burkina Faso | CFA franc | Peg to euro | Yes | 1996 |
| Côte d'Ivoire | CFA franc | Peg to euro | Yes | 1996 |
| Guinea-Bissau | CFA franc | Peg to euro | Yes | 1997 |
| Mali | CFA franc | Peg to euro | Yes | 1996 |
| Niger | CFA franc | Peg to euro | Yes | 1996 |
| Senegal | CFA franc | Peg to euro | Yes | 1996 |
| Togo | CFA franc | Peg to euro | Yes | 1996 |
| **Other ECOWAS** | | | | |
| Cape Verde | Cape Verde escudo | Peg to euro | No | |
| Gambia, The | Dalasi | Independent float | Yes | 1993 |
| Ghana | Cedi | Independent float | Yes | 1994 |
| Guinea | Guinean franc | Independent float | Yes | 1995 |
| Liberia | Liberian dollar | Independent float | No | |
| Nigeria | Naira | Managed float[1] | No[2] | |
| Sierra Leone | Leone | Independent float | Yes | 1995 |

[1] With no preannounced path for the exchange rate.
[2] While not yet formalized by acceptance of Article VIII of the IMF's Articles of Agreement, current account restrictions have been lifted, in practice.

- The extent to which the exchange rates are currently market-determined varies significantly across countries. Central banks often intervene heavily to manage the exchange rate.
- Since the exchange rate is no longer the nominal anchor for price stability, governments have chosen various forms of monetary nominal anchors. The root causes of losses of control over inflation, however, have come from the inability to shield the central bank from weak fiscal discipline or from losses of fiscal control in the face of shocks.
- Most of the countries achieved significant depreciations of the real effective exchange rate following the adoption of reform programs. In recent years, however, real effective exchange rates have either fluctuated around a constant trend or appreciated, implying that for some countries, competitiveness relative to the WAEMU countries following the 1994 CFA franc devaluation has eroded.
- More flexible exchange rate arrangements have allowed adjustment of real effective exchange rates to terms of trade movements with fewer periods of serious misalignment.
- Institutionally, many countries have moved to market-determined rates and foreign exchange allocation through interbank markets. The development of efficient interbank markets, however, has been hindered by structural problems in the financial sector: small market size, limited competition across banks (including in some cases collusion), government involvement or management of banks, limited financial instruments, and solvency and liquidity problems.
- Thin markets can lead to excessive volatility of the exchange rate with negative consequences for real sector activities. Central banks seem to have made some progress in intervening to smooth fluctuations. (Potential trade-offs between exchange rate volatility and interest rate volatility can arise, however.)
- Heavy intervention to resist nominal depreciation can create problems of high domestic interest rates, which add to the fiscal costs of servicing domestic debt and can have negative consequences for economic activity.
- Policymakers operating in flexible exchange rate systems perceive that there is a policy dilemma in terms of maintaining a competitive exchange rate and, at the same time, avoiding acceleration and instability in inflation. Although cognizant of the need to allow the exchange rate to depreciate in response to market forces so that the real effective exchange rate is maintained at a competitive level, policymakers are often concerned that rapid nominal depreciation will ignite inflation.

In sum, neither pegged rates nor flexible rates on their own provide an easy solution for the major policy challenges facing countries in the region. Neither option is a panacea. A pegged rate (to the French franc) in WAEMU led to large overvaluations and severe recession in the late 1980s and early 1990s. By allowing a measure of flexibility in response to severe terms of trade shocks, flexible rates have cushioned some of the negative effects on output. They often have not been managed in a disciplined way, however, and as a result, they often have been accompanied by exchange rate instability and high inflation.

# IV  What Is a Monetary Union?

A monetary union is a zone where a single monetary policy prevails and inside which a single currency, or currencies which are perfect substitutes, circulate freely. Most countries issue their own currencies that are not linked to others and thus constitute monetary unions on their own. However, this chapter examines only the cases of monetary unions that extend across national borders to a group of sovereign countries. Lessons are drawn from their experience in the next chapter.

Polly Reynolds Allen (1976, p. 4) distinguishes between those elements that *define* a monetary union and those additional characteristics that are necessary for the continued and successful existence of the monetary union. A monetary union is defined by the following characteristics: (1) a single money, or several currencies fully convertible at immutably fixed exchange rates; (2) an arrangement whereby monetary policy is determined at the union level, allowing no national autonomy in monetary policy; and (3) a single external exchange rate policy ("Toward this end, national authorities must relinquish individual control over their international reserves and invest such control in a union authority," Allen, 1976, p. 4).

A related concept is "monetary integration." A monetary union is an example of full (or nearly full) monetary integration. Monetary integration has been defined by Max Corden as involving two components: "*exchange-rate union,* that is, an area within which exchange rates bear a permanently fixed relationship to each other . . ." and "*convertibility*—the permanent absence of all exchange controls, whether for current or capital transactions, within the area" (Corden, 1972, p. 2). He goes on to distinguish a true exchange rate union from a "pseudo-exchange rate union," where there is an agreement to maintain fixed exchange rates but "there is no explicit integration of economic policy, no common pool of foreign-exchange reserves, and no single central bank" (Corden, 1972, p. 3). Since the tools for maintaining exchange rates permanently fixed do not exist in a pseudo-exchange rate union, there is always the possibility that one or another country would find it expedient to allow its rate to depreciate or appreciate against the others. The expectation that this may occur will interfere with the smooth operation of monetary union and prevent complete monetary integration. Similarly, Cobham and Robson (1994) distinguish between formal and informal monetary unions; the latter are not completely credible and hence, in their view, have drawbacks relative to formal monetary unions.

Thus, all the above authors stress the need for institutional safeguards to ensure that there will be a single monetary policy and, if there is more than a single currency, an irrevocable fixation of exchange rates. The need for such guarantees explains why the authors believe that the continued existence of national central banks and national currencies casts some doubt on the permanence of the union: they make exit from the union too easy. Similarly, pooling of reserves is viewed as essential to ensure a common external policy for the currency union.

More fundamentally, the permanence of a monetary union requires a strong bond of solidarity among member countries. Cohen (1998, p. 87) argues that in the absence of a dominant power with an interest in making the arrangement function effectively on terms acceptable to all, there must be a genuine sense of community among the partners. This sense of community may be the result of a long period of close cooperation and it may be manifested by other institutions that enable each member to benefit from assistance from the others if suffering unfavorable circumstances. Cohen points to cases where the absence of a hegemonic power or of solidarity among members led monetary unions to fail.

In order to get the widest possible benefits of a common currency as a means of payment, convertibility within the area is essential. Typically, enlarging a currency's area of circulation is a key objective of monetary union, but this is only useful if the currency can fully serve as a means of payment; that is, the currency is internally convertible within the region. *External* convertibility also enhances the usefulness of the currency for residents of the monetary union, since restrictions on the ability to acquire foreign currency to make external transactions may provide incentives for domestic residents to hold foreign currencies (legally or illegally). External convertibility is not a defining feature of a monetary union, however.

The function of a currency as a store of value (and ultimately as a medium of exchange) depends on the currency keeping its value in terms of goods and services against which it is exchanged. This, in turn, requires an institutional setting in which the responsibility for the single monetary policy of the currency area is clearly established, the mandate is given to the central bank to maintain the value of the currency, and the central bank is granted the independence and tools for achieving that mandate. In particular, the common monetary policy must not allow for uncontrolled sources of monetary expansion nor should the central bank be subject to pressures to provide direct financing of government deficits or indirect financing through the banking system. The central bank must be able to alter the quantity of high powered money and the level of interest rates in order to control monetary expansion and achieve price stability.

# V    Lessons from the Experience of Currency Unions

Existing currency unions can shed some light on the requirements for making a monetary union function smoothly and hence on desirable features of a possible currency union in West Africa. In this regard, it is also useful to survey the experience of other currency unions that have not survived.

Presently, there are only five unions and among them the WAEMU currency area is the most directly relevant for ECOWAS since the eight WAEMU members are also ECOWAS members. Appendix III surveys the extensive literature on the effect of a common currency on the economic performance of WAEMU countries and the countries making up the other CFA franc zone in Central Africa, the Central African Economic and Monetary Community (CAEMC). The currency of both zones is convertible into French francs (and, since 1999, the euro) at a parity that is guaranteed by the French Treasury.

A third currency area, the Eastern Caribbean Currency Union (ECCU) is constituted by eight small island economies that share a single currency, the Eastern Caribbean dollar, and a central bank, the Eastern Caribbean Central Bank (ECCB). As in the case of the CFA franc zones, this currency area is a legacy of a colonial monetary arrangement and it operates as a quasi-currency board. However, it provides an example of a union with a strong external peg (the exchange rate against the U.S. dollar has remained unchanged since 1976), maintained purely through regional discipline and available reserves, rather than through an external guarantee.

Fourth, the Common Monetary Area (CMA) is constituted by South Africa and three smaller countries grouped around it: Lesotho, Namibia, and Swaziland. Given the dominant size of South Africa, this currency area uses the rand, although the other countries retain their own currencies, which are pegged to the rand.

The fifth currency area is the most recent and by far the most economically important—namely, the euro area. Although the euro has been in existence only since January 1, 1999, the European Union's extensive process of institutional preparation for a new central bank and a new currency, as well as the efforts invested in convergence, provide important lessons for the creation *de novo* of a currency area.

In addition to considering existing currency areas, we also draw lessons from failed currency areas. We consider the breakdown of the ruble zone after the dissolution of the Soviet Union, which illustrates the pitfalls of inadequate institutional safeguards, and the currency area constituted by the East African Community (EAC) in the 1970s, which failed from lack of member solidarity and uncoordinated monetary expansion.

A detailed description of each of the five currency areas (as well as the ruble zone, the EAC, and several cases where the currency of a large country serves as legal tender in a smaller neighbor) is given in Appendix II, while essential features of existing currency areas are summarized in Table 5.1. The table suggests considerable diversity across monetary unions. The CMA is the weakest institutionally, in that separate currencies and central banks make the internal exchange rates revocable and dissolution of the currency union is itself relatively easy. This monetary area would be termed a "pseudo currency union" by Corden and doubts about its continued existence are consistent with Allen's analysis. Indeed, Tjirongo (1998) questions whether the full credibility advantages of membership accrue to Namibia, given the union's revocable nature. The euro area is the strongest, given the size of regional trade and the fact that it has followed the creation of other institutions manifesting regional solidarity and linking the countries together in numerous ways.

A *first* lesson is that a true monetary union must be accompanied by the creation of a single institution with clear assignment of responsibility for formulating and conducting monetary policy. Decentralized decision making is not possible in the context of a monetary union. The "free rider problem" is well illustrated by the experience of the ruble zone. With the dissolution of the Soviet Union, the newly independent republics had some autonomy in money creation and most proceeded to extract seigniorage as quickly as possible, taking advantage of mechanisms that allowed them to borrow without limit from the Central Bank of Russia. Accelerating inflation was the result. The instability of the ruble and its failure to provide both the monetary services of a means of

### Table 5.1. Characteristics of Monetary Unions

|  | ECCU | WAEMU | CAEMC | Euro Area | CMA |
|---|---|---|---|---|---|
| Number of countries | 8 | 8 | 6 | 12 | 4 |
| Single currency? | Yes (EC$) | Yes (CFA franc) | Yes (CFA franc) | Yes (euro)[1] | No (but rand circulates in all) |
| Single central bank? | Yes (ECCB) | Yes (BCEAO) | Yes (BEAC) | No (but ECB sets monetary policy) | No (but South African Reserve Bank sets monetary policy) |
| Common pool of reserves? | Yes | Yes | Yes | Yes | No |
| Free trade area? | No | No | No | Yes | Yes (SACU) |
| Common external tariff? | No | Yes | Yes, in principle | Yes | Yes (SACU) |
| Share of internal to total trade[2] | <10 | 9.5 | 3.3 | 46 | ... |
| External current account convertibility? | Yes | Yes (assured by French Treasury) | Yes (assured by French Treasury) | Yes | Yes |
| Degree of capital mobility within region | Moderate | Low, though in principle free | Low, though in principle free | High | High |
| External exchange rate anchor? | Yes (peg to US$) | Yes (peg to FF/euro) | Yes (peg to FF/euro) | No | No |
| Ratio of per capita GDP of richest to poorest | 3.2 | 4.7 | 20 | 4.0 | 8.1 |
| Similarity of exports | High | Medium | Low | High | Medium |

[1]The euro, the single European currency, will replace the national currencies of 12 member countries of the European Union over a three-and-a-half-year period that began on January 1, 1999. (Greece joined the initial group of 11 countries on January 1, 2001.) The euro area's national currencies and the euro will coexist until mid-2002.
[2]Based on data for 1998 in IMF, *Direction of Trade Statistics*.

payment (it was not generally convertible against goods within the ruble zone) and a store of value quickly made it unattractive as a common currency. In the EAC, the tight controls on monetary expansion embodied in the currency board were progressively loosened, as member governments succeeded in expanding the amount of direct and indirect financing extended to them by their national central banks.

Decentralized execution of monetary policy, if accompanied by tight controls on monetary expansion or intervention, is, however, possible in principle, but the euro zone is unique in this respect. In the European Union (EU), it was decided to retain national central banks along with the new European Central Bank (ECB) as part of the European System of Central Banks. The ECB has a monopoly over monetary policy, however, and the tight constraints prohibiting any direct or indirect financing of governments make any attempts by national central banks at circumventing the ECB's monetary policy improbable.

A *second* important lesson for the successful operation of a monetary union is that the central bank must be free from pressures to finance governments, whether directly or indirectly. Although the CFA zones respected formal limits on monetary financing, there were enough loopholes that some of the national governments managed to extract seigniorage. Specifically, because certain types of central bank loans were not subject to the ceilings, national governments induced their commercial banks to borrow from the central bank and then to transfer the funds to the governments, which used the proceeds for their own purposes. The banking crises that occurred in the 1980s in most countries of both WAEMU and CAEMC resulted, and the central banks of the two zones ended up bailing out insolvent institutions. In the end, the governments of the largest countries (Côte d'Ivoire and Cameroon, respectively) managed to appropriate a disproportionate amount of seigniorage through this process (Stasavage, 1996).

It is clear that neither monetary union nor pegged exchange rates per se are sufficient to discipline fiscal policy, as the CFA example shows. In fact, some have argued (e.g., Tornell and Velasco, 1995) that flexible rates may provide a more immediate signal

# V  LESSONS FROM THE EXPERIENCE OF CURRENCY UNIONS

of overexpansionary fiscal policies and make policy mistakes more visible. Therefore, a currency union needs reinforced surveillance over fiscal policies of its members, accompanied by effective sanctions and close supervision of banks. The fear of pressures on the European Central Bank explains the great pains taken in Europe not only to rule out monetary financing, but also to control excessive deficits.

A *third* lesson, or at least empirical regularity, is that monetary unions have usually been organized around a strong existing central bank or through a peg to a stable international currency. This is true of the CFA franc zones and the ECCU, and also of the euro zone, where the Deutsche Bundesbank (German central bank) provided the model of monetary stability. In some cases, asymmetry in the size of the countries concerned has given the large country effective control over the monetary union (e.g., South Africa in the rand area and the United States for Panama's monetary policy). The more symmetric monetary unions with weaker intraregional institutions have relied on an external anchor: for example, in the ECCU, the peg was to the pound sterling and later to the U.S. dollar; WAEMU and CAEMC peg to the French franc (and, since 1999, to the euro). In contrast, the ruble zone at the break up of the Soviet Union had neither a strong stability-oriented institution at its center nor an external anchor.

*Fourth,* even long-standing monetary unions need not lead to strong regional integration in other dimensions, such as strong regional trade links or other regional institutions. For instance, the ECCU, WAEMU, and CAEMC all have relatively low internal trade. Empirical literature surveyed in Appendix III suggests that currency unions do provide some stimulus to trade, with a recent (high) estimate of the effect implying that membership increases trade by as much as a factor of three. However, the still relatively low level of internal trade has stimulated other initiatives in WAEMU—in particular, the creation of a common external tariff, indirect tax harmonization, standardization of business law, and the formation of a regional stock exchange. In both ECCU and CAEMC, monetary union has been accompanied by a lesser development of regional institutions. Conversely, strong trade ties do not have to be accompanied by monetary union or even fixed exchange rates. A notable example is the North American Free Trade Agreement (NAFTA), where Canada and Mexico are the United States' main trading partners, and vice versa, although their currencies float against the U.S. dollar.

A *fifth* lesson is that the evidence is mixed on whether monetary union is an important stimulus to growth. Evidence from the CFA franc zones initially suggested a positive impact relative to the rest of sub-Saharan Africa (e.g., Guillaumont and Guillaumont, 1984; Devarajan and de Melo, 1987). As indicated in chapter III, however, these zones severely underperformed in the 1986–93 period.[17] Frankel and Rose (2000) argue that currency unions promote growth through increased intraregional trade and Guillaumont, Guillaumont-Jeanneney, and Brun (1999) point to instability (including price instability, which should be reduced by monetary union) as a factor reducing African growth. However, it is clear that monetary policy on its own cannot ensure sustained growth without favorable real conditions in the economy, including more fundamental determinants of growth that include sound fiscal and structural policies, and trade liberalization.

*Sixth,* the existing currency unions that we have surveyed have all been associated with low inflation, but this is in no way guaranteed, as the example of the ruble zone indicates. Price stability is less a feature of currency unions per se than of the way that monetary policy is anchored and whether there are adequate safeguards against excessive monetary expansion. Inflation has been lower in CFA franc countries than in the rest of sub-Saharan Africa, but it is difficult to disentangle the effects of the discipline provided by the CFA franc's link to the French franc, the indirect influence of France's convertibility guarantee on the monetary policies of the CFA franc zone, and the effect of monetary union among WAEMU or CAEMC countries per se. Again, the ECCU has recorded low inflation, resulting from a peg to a strong currency. Except for the CMA, there are no examples of existing monetary unions among developing countries that do not anchor to an industrial country currency; therefore, it is hard to determine whether such a strategy is likely to be successful in bringing to bear greater monetary discipline than each country could achieve on its own.

However, there are two examples of failed monetary unions that did not have such an anchor. The ruble zone, which was centered on an inconvertible currency without an anchor to an international currency, collapsed amidst high inflation, but this was due to lack of structures for controlling monetary growth and in the context of a breakdown of existing political ties. The monetary union in the East African Community also broke down as a result of lack of effective supranational controls on national monetary creation. Indeed, Guillaume and Stasavage (2000) argue that successful monetary unions must be accompanied by parallel regional arrangements and/or links to financial and technical assistance of industrial countries that make it costly to violate the rules of the monetary union or to withdraw from it.

---

[17]This may have partly resulted from the peg to the French franc (which appreciated against the U.S. dollar over the period), rather than the monetary union among *African* countries.

# VI  The Benefits and Costs of a Common Currency for West Africa

There is an extensive literature concerning the advisability for a given country of joining a monetary union.[18] There are two general issues that should influence the choice. A first issue is whether the economic structures of candidates to join a monetary union are similar enough or flexible enough to support a fixed exchange rate between their currencies. A second issue is whether the institutions created to carry out the common monetary policy are likely to lead to improved policies. It is important to distinguish these two issues because a monetary union goes beyond simply fixing exchange rates between member countries. It is also important to distinguish between monetary union among a set of countries, thus tying their currencies together, and the *external* exchange rate policy of the union (e.g., whether to peg to the U.S. dollar or the euro).

For instance, the Ghanaian currency (cedi) could be pegged to the Nigerian currency (naira), through the intervention of Ghana's central bank (and/or Nigeria's central bank), but Ghana would retain its own currency and the possibility of changing its parity. Monetary union would be more constraining than a pegged rate because it would involve the irrevocable fixing of the cedi/naira parity and also would require institutions for carrying out a common monetary and exchange rate policy. The common currency could be pegged or could fluctuate against major currencies, with a greater or lesser amount of official intervention on the part of the union's central bank, depending on the external exchange rate policy.

For a monetary union to be desirable, the basic criteria for a fixed exchange rate between the two currencies must be satisfied. In addition, there must be a willingness to give up the possibility of any adjustment of parities (except if the monetary union is abandoned), and a political commitment to enter into close ties with the other countries of the monetary union. Because of the stronger constraints involved in monetary union, it may have greater benefits than a fixed rate alone. In particular, it may provide a more effective way of tying the hands of the monetary authorities (to provide an "agency of restraint" in Paul Collier's words), and may stimulate trade and promote other aspects of regional integration.

## Benefits of a Fixed Exchange Rate Relationship

The benefits of a fixed rate between countries of a monetary union tend to be greater if the countries concerned already have a substantial amount of trade among themselves, since transactions costs and bilateral exchange rate fluctuations related to that trade will be reduced. The more asymmetric (and large) the shocks facing the countries, the greater are the costs of a fixed rate, increasing the attraction of retaining an independent monetary and exchange rate policy. Countries are less likely to face large asymmetric terms of trade shocks if they have diversified economies with similar structures. For instance, a country that exports oil and imports mainly manufactures is likely to experience different movements in its terms of trade than a country exporting cocoa and importing oil. Asymmetry of shocks will be less of a problem if there is substantial labor mobility or there exists a system of fiscal transfers across the region.

How do the countries of ECOWAS fare on the basis of these criteria?

### Trade Patterns

Table 6.1 summarizes the trade patterns for ECOWAS countries. Internal trade within the region is relatively small, at a little over 10 percent of the average of exports and imports. Unfortunately, official statistics do not incorporate informal trade,

---

[18]Much of this literature was written in the context of European monetary integration, although Robert Mundell's seminal article (Mundell, 1961), which launched the idea of "optimum currency areas," referred to Canada and the United States. It needs to be recognized that the various criteria for optimum currency areas do not have much predictive power when it comes to actual exchange rate regimes. In addition, as noted by Frankel and Rose (1998), these criteria are to some extent endogenous: membership in a monetary union may help make the shocks hitting member countries more symmetric and also expand intra-union trade.

# VI  THE BENEFITS AND COSTS OF A COMMON CURRENCY FOR WEST AFRICA

**Table 6.1. ECOWAS: Patterns of Trade**
(1997–98 average)

|  | Exports (Percent of total exports) | Imports (Percent of total imports) |
|---|---|---|
| **ECOWAS countries** | | |
| ECOWAS | 8.4 | 13.1 |
| European Union | 42.3 | 43.3 |
| Rest of the world | 49.3 | 43.6 |
| **WAEMU countries** | | |
| WAEMU | 7.3 | 11.2 |
| Other ECOWAS | 4.6 | 6.2 |
| European Union | 29.9 | 40.3 |
| Rest of the world | 58.2 | 42.3 |
| **Non-WAEMU countries** | | |
| Non-WAEMU | 1.5 | 3.2 |
| WAEMU | 3.0 | 5.0 |
| European Union | 56.4 | 46.7 |
| Rest of the world | 39.1 | 45.1 |

Source: IMF, *Direction of Trade Statistics*, 1999.

which is thought to be considerable and to reflect efforts to avoid trade restrictions and trade taxes, as well as the difficulty in acquiring convertible currencies. Under-reporting of intra-union trade may also reflect traditional trade patterns (e.g., between coastal states and the Sahel) that are not picked up in the official statistics. Estimates of informal trade suggest that, if it were included, intra-ECOWAS trade might be increased by several percentage points. In any case, the aggregate figure hides quite different behavior for WAEMU countries and the remaining countries. The former countries trade considerably more among themselves than do the non-WAEMU, ECOWAS countries.[19] The EU is the largest trading partner of the countries in the region, accounting for more than 40 percent of the region's total exports and imports.

## Asymmetry of Shocks

An important source of shocks, especially for countries whose exports are primary commodities, is the terms of trade. Figure 6.1 presents the evolution of the terms of trade for each of the region's economies, while Table 6.2 calculates the correlations of changes in those terms of trade. Several features stand out.

*First*, there are very large movements of the terms of trade for several of the countries. The amplitude of the swings is especially large for Nigeria and the swings are related in large part to changes in the world price of oil, Nigeria's major export. Other countries also face large changes in the terms of trade; those in Côte d'Ivoire and Ghana, for instance, are substantially related to the world price of cocoa.

*Second*, these shocks to the terms of trade are typically not well correlated, due in large part to differences in commodity exports, and the fact that the world prices of the various commodities do not move together. Although some primary commodities are common to a number of countries in the region—coffee, cocoa, cotton, fish products, timber, and groundnuts—others are found in only one or two countries (bauxite in Guinea, phosphate in Senegal and Togo, uranium in Niger, and oil in Nigeria). Nigeria, Guinea, Niger, and Guinea-Bissau are each dependent on a single commodity for 50 percent or more of their export earnings (Cashin and Pattillo, 2000). Nigeria is a substantial oil exporter, while most of the other countries of the region are net oil importers. As a result, Nigeria's terms of trade changes are substantially negatively correlated with those of Côte d'Ivoire, Niger, Ghana, Liberia, and Sierra Leone, and either weakly negatively or weakly positively correlated with the rest, except for Guinea.

*Third*, the correlations tend to be higher for the WAEMU countries among themselves than either the correlation of WAEMU with non-WAEMU countries or the correlations among non-WAEMU countries.

A broader assessment of the possibility for asymmetric shocks hitting the economies of the region can be obtained by comparing production structures. The production structure (Table 6.3) is quite varied across countries. While most are heavily agricultural, the share of agriculture in GDP in 1997 ranges from 54 percent (Guinea-Bissau) to 9 percent (Cape Verde). There are large differences in the share of manufacturing in GDP, with Burkina Faso (18 percent), Côte d'Ivoire (18 percent), Senegal (15 percent), and Ghana (10 percent) having the largest shares.

## Labor Mobility

Hard data on labor mobility are difficult to obtain. However, it seems likely that mobility is high between some countries of the region and follows traditional migratory and trading patterns that cut across national boundaries, for instance between the Sahel and coastal areas. According to World Bank estimates, the countries having the largest proportions of resident foreigners in ECOWAS are Côte

---

[19]The evidence that internal WAEMU trade is higher as a result of the common currency is surveyed in Appendix III. Bilateral trade among ECOWAS countries is expected to be small, given the small size of their economies and low per capita income.

# Benefits of a Fixed Exchange Rate Relationship

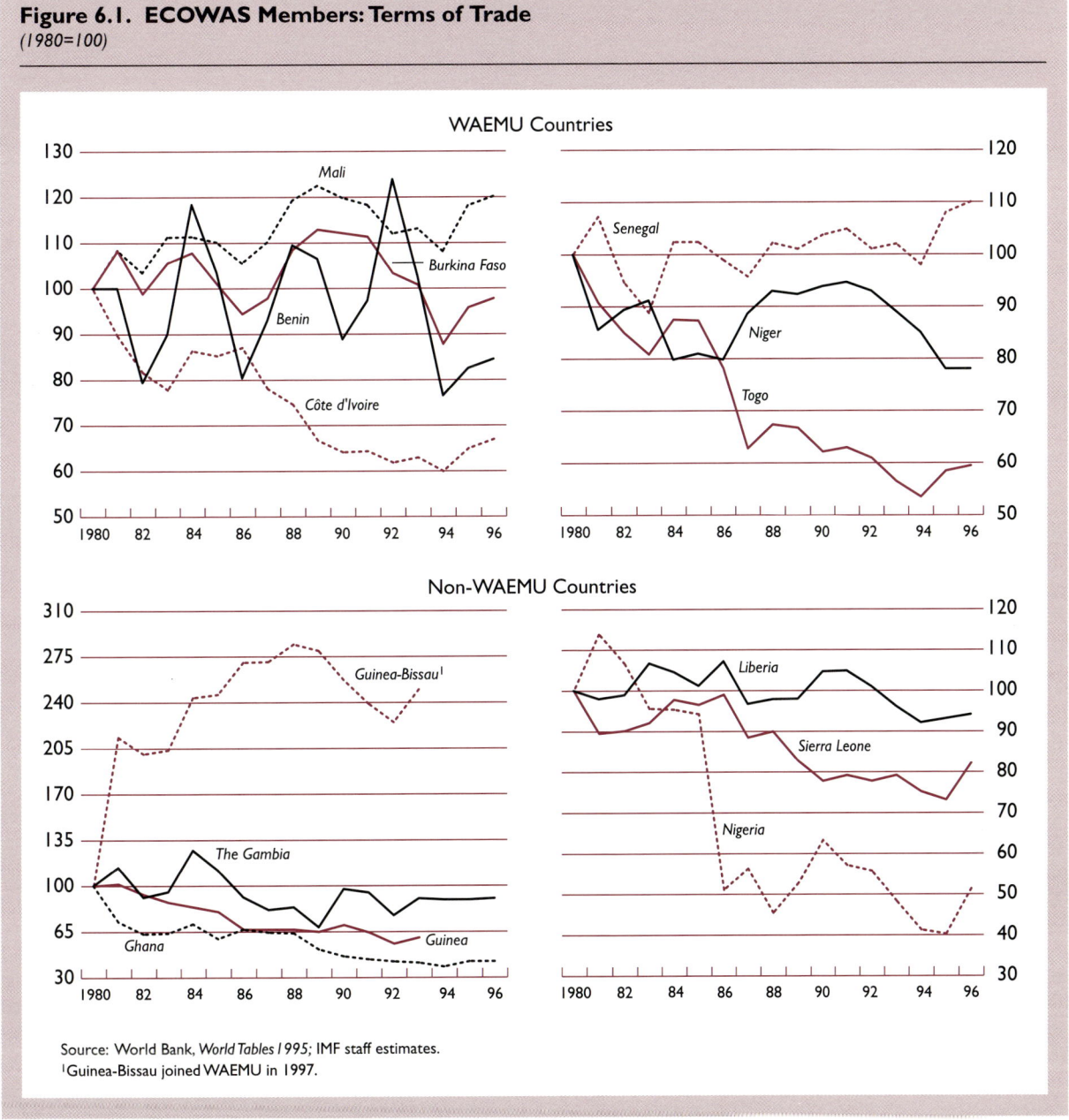

**Figure 6.1. ECOWAS Members: Terms of Trade**
(1980=100)

Source: World Bank, *World Tables 1995*; IMF staff estimates.
[1] Guinea-Bissau joined WAEMU in 1997.

d'Ivoire (26 percent), The Gambia (14 percent), and Guinea (8 percent) (World Bank, 2000). ECOWAS has facilitated mobility by eliminating visa requirements, but citizens of one ECOWAS country seeking to establish residency in another ECOWAS country still seem to encounter administrative difficulties.

### Fiscal Transfers

Federal or unitary states that constitute monetary unions have a mechanism that helps to cushion different shocks hitting different regions. In Europe, the absence of fiscal federalism among countries has been viewed as a considerable drawback to the sustainability of monetary union (Sala-i-Martin and Sachs, 1992). Although it does not have a federal system of taxes and transfers, the EU has set up a "Cohesion Fund" that is designed to subsidize poorer regions.

The six non-WAEMU countries in ECOWAS have announced their intention to set up a Stabilization and Cooperation Fund to make temporary transfers among the converging economies of the mone-

# VI THE BENEFITS AND COSTS OF A COMMON CURRENCY FOR WEST AFRICA

**Table 6.2. ECOWAS Members: Correlation of Changes in Terms of Trade**
(1980–96)

| | Benin | Burkina Faso | Côte d'Ivoire | Mali | Niger | Senegal | Togo | The Gambia | Ghana | Guinea | Guinea-Bissau | Liberia | Nigeria | Sierra Leone |
|---|---|---|---|---|---|---|---|---|---|---|---|---|---|---|
| Benin | | 0.56* | 0.22 | 0.43** | –0.03 | 0.46** | 0.28 | 0.14 | 0.33 | –0.19 | 0.07 | –0.09 | 0.07 | 0.19 |
| Burkina Faso | 0.56* | | 0.06 | 0.94* | –0.02 | 0.57* | 0.11 | 0.37 | 0.16 | 0.26 | 0.50** | 0.29 | 0.02 | 0.06 |
| Côte d'Ivoire | 0.22 | 0.06 | | –0.01 | –0.40** | 0.59* | 0.52* | 0.36 | 0.75* | –0.16 | –0.13 | 0.17 | –0.23 | 0.65* |
| Mali | 0.43** | 0.94* | –0.01 | | –0.06 | 0.48* | 0.07 | 0.26 | 0.08 | 0.32 | 0.54* | 0.16 | 0.01 | –0.05 |
| Niger | –0.03 | –0.02 | –0.40** | –0.06 | | –0.57* | –0.41** | –0.31 | 0.05 | –0.13 | –0.55* | 0.10 | –0.17 | 0.06 |
| Senegal | 0.46** | 0.57* | 0.59* | 0.48* | –0.57* | | 0.49* | 0.62* | 0.28 | 0.33 | 0.45* | 0.00 | 0.09 | 0.15 |
| Togo | 0.28 | 0.11 | 0.52* | 0.07 | –0.41** | 0.49* | | 0.03 | 0.14 | 0.07 | –0.29 | 0.01 | 0.27 | 0.26 |
| Gambia, The | 0.14 | 0.37 | 0.36 | 0.26 | –0.31 | 0.62* | 0.03 | | 0.17 | 0.54* | 0.33 | 0.29 | 0.06 | 0.17 |
| Ghana | 0.33 | 0.16 | 0.75* | 0.08 | 0.05 | 0.28 | 0.14 | 0.17 | | –0.41 | –0.27 | 0.31 | –0.54* | 0.62* |
| Guinea | –0.19 | 0.26 | –0.16 | 0.32 | –0.13 | 0.33 | 0.07 | 0.54* | –0.41 | | 0.09 | –0.29 | 0.59* | –0.44 |
| Guinea-Bissau | 0.07 | 0.50** | –0.13 | 0.54* | –0.55* | 0.45** | –0.29 | 0.33 | –0.27 | 0.09 | | 0.03 | –0.09 | –0.16 |
| Liberia | –0.09 | 0.29 | 0.17 | 0.16 | 0.10 | 0.00 | 0.01 | 0.29 | 0.31 | –0.29 | 0.03 | | –0.38 | 0.43** |
| Nigeria | 0.07 | 0.02 | –0.23 | 0.01 | –0.17 | 0.09 | 0.27 | 0.06 | –0.54* | 0.59* | –0.09 | –0.38 | | –0.38 |
| Sierra Leone | 0.19 | 0.06 | 0.65* | –0.05 | 0.06 | 0.15 | 0.26 | 0.17 | 0.62* | –0.44 | –0.16 | 0.43** | –0.38 | |
| Average All | 0.19 | 0.30 | 0.18 | 0.24 | –0.19 | 0.30 | 0.12 | 0.23 | 0.13 | 0.04 | 0.04 | 0.08 | –0.05 | 0.12 |
| Average WAEMU[1] | 0.32 | 0.37 | 0.16 | 0.31 | –0.25 | 0.34 | 0.17 | 0.21 | 0.26 | 0.07 | 0.08 | 0.09 | 0.01 | 0.19 |
| Average Non-WAEMU | 0.07 | 0.24 | 0.20 | 0.19 | –0.14 | 0.27 | 0.07 | 0.26 | –0.02 | 0.01 | –0.01 | 0.06 | –0.12 | 0.04 |

Source: Calculated from the Terms of Trade Index (1987=100, U.S. dollar based), from World Bank, *World Tables 1995*.
* Significant at 5 percent level.
** Significant at 10 percent level.
[1] Guinea-Bissau is not included with WAEMU above because the country was not a member of WAEMU during the 1980–96 period covered in the table.

tary union.[20] Details on how the fund would function await the results of a study to be prepared by the ECOWAS Technical Committee on the West African Monetary Zone. According to the ECOWAS Task Force assisting the Technical Committee, the fund will begin operating once 75 percent of the proposed initial capital amount of US$50 million has been raised. It is envisaged that no country would be permitted to borrow more than 25 percent of the fund's proposed total resources of US$100 million. Countries seeking to draw on fund resources reportedly would be obliged to submit applications that would indicate proposed measures for addressing the adjustment problems caused by shocks to their economies.

Notably, for such a fund to operate, the commitment of each country to help its neighbors must be strong. In the past, some countries have not paid their dues to the ECOWAS institutions for many years. In addition, given the size of Nigeria relative to its neighbors, the operation of such a fund may well be asymmetric. Transfers to the smaller countries encountering difficulties could be sizable, but if Nigeria were to draw it could quickly exhaust resources available from the fund.

## Conditions for Monetary Stability of the Currency Union

A currency union requires an investment in the institutions necessary to guarantee irrevocably fixed exchange rates and a single monetary policy. A single monetary policy has several different implications. On the one hand, it further reduces nominal flexibility relative to fixed but adjustable exchange rates. On the other hand, supranational institutions may constitute an "agency of restraint," so that monetary union can improve the stability of monetary policy, provided the central bank is given the independence and instruments that allow it to achieve its objectives. To achieve the benefits of monetary union, however, the political commitment must exist, as well as a considerable degree of solidarity among the countries of the union; otherwise, the monetary union will not be credible or durable. As in the EU context, commitment to a stable monetary union and an independent central bank can best be demonstrated by achievement of "convergence criteria" at the national level. The ECOWAS countries planning the "second monetary union" have intro-

---

[20]"ECOWAS Monetary Zone: Compensation Fund Underway," *This Day* (Lagos), July 10, 2000, and ECOWAS Press Releases No. 94/2000 and No. 98/2000. As noted above, WAEMU has already established structural funds for subregional development.

## Table 6.3. ECOWAS Members: Production Structure

| | 1978 | 1988 | 1997 | | 1978 | 1988 | 1997 |
|---|---|---|---|---|---|---|---|
| | *(As a percentage share of GDP)* | | | | *(As a percentage share of GDP)* | | |
| **Benin** | | | | **Liberia** | | | |
| Agriculture | 34.5 | 34.7 | 38.3 | Agriculture | 30.5 | ... | ... |
| Industry | 14.0 | 13.4 | 13.8 | Industry | 26.2 | ... | ... |
|   Manufacturing | 10.8 | 8.0 | 8.2 |   Manufacturing | 5.7 | ... | ... |
| Services, etc. | 51.5 | 51.9 | 47.9 | Services, etc. | 32.3 | ... | ... |
| **Burkina Faso** | | | | **Mali** | | | |
| Agriculture | 34.0 | 31.4 | 32.6 | Agriculture | 55.3 | 42.6 | 46.9 |
| Industry | 22.9 | 22.2 | 23.8 | Industry | 10.4 | 15.0 | 16.5 |
|   Manufacturing | 15.9 | 16.5 | 18.1 |   Manufacturing | 5.1 | 8.4 | 6.7 |
| Services, etc. | 37.2 | 42.2 | 37.8 | Services, etc. | 29.1 | 37.1 | 32.0 |
| **Cape Verde** | | | | **Niger** | | | |
| Agriculture | ... | 18.3 | 8.7 | Agriculture | 52.7 | 35.4 | 38.2 |
| Industry | ... | 27.0 | 21.4 | Industry | 15.0 | 17.4 | 18.0 |
|   Manufacturing | ... | ... | 0.5 |   Manufacturing | 4.6 | 5.9 | 6.5 |
| Services, etc. | ... | 54.7 | 69.9 | Services, etc. | 32.4 | 47.3 | 43.7 |
| **Côte d'Ivoire** | | | | **Nigeria** | | | |
| Agriculture | 25.9 | 32.0 | 27.3 | Agriculture | 29.9 | 39.9 | 31.7 |
| Industry | 16.5 | 22.7 | 21.2 | Industry | 32.7 | 30.3 | 45.3 |
|   Manufacturing | 7.7 | 19.5 | 17.6 |   Manufacturing | 6.4 | 7.4 | 4.6 |
| Services, etc. | 57.6 | 45.3 | 51.5 | Services, etc. | 35.5 | 28.1 | 19.8 |
| **Gambia, The** | | | | **Senegal** | | | |
| Agriculture | 27.9 | 27.4 | 25.9 | Agriculture | 20.8 | 22.4 | 18.4 |
| Industry | 10.6 | 9.5 | 12.8 | Industry | 15.0 | 18.4 | 22.2 |
|   Manufacturing | 3.8 | 4.8 | 5.3 |   Manufacturing | ... | 13.3 | 14.7 |
| Services, etc. | 48.4 | 51.1 | 48.1 | Services, etc. | 64.2 | 59.1 | 59.4 |
| **Ghana** | | | | **Sierra Leone** | | | |
| Agriculture | 60.7 | 49.6 | 47.4 | Agriculture | 34.2 | 51.1 | ... |
| Industry | 12.0 | 16.6 | 16.6 | Industry | 20.8 | 15.4 | ... |
|   Manufacturing | 8.6 | 9.6 | 9.5 |   Manufacturing | 5.5 | 4.6 | ... |
| Services, etc. | 27.3 | 33.8 | 36.0 | Services, etc. | 42.8 | 28.8 | ... |
| **Guinea** | | | | **Togo** | | | |
| Agriculture | ... | 23.3 | 24.1 | Agriculture | 24.1 | 33.6 | 41.8 |
| Industry | ... | 33.4 | 33.0 | Industry | 22.8 | 21.5 | 20.8 |
|   Manufacturing | ... | 4.5 | 4.5 |   Manufacturing | 5.9 | 7.7 | 8.7 |
| Services, etc. | ... | 43.3 | 42.9 | Services, etc. | 53.1 | 44.9 | 37.4 |
| **Guinea-Bissau** | | | | | | | |
| Agriculture | 51.6 | 54.0 | 53.8 | | | | |
| Industry | 20.0 | 13.5 | 11.0 | | | | |
|   Manufacturing | ... | 6.0 | 7.0 | | | | |
| Services, etc. | 28.4 | 32.5 | 35.1 | | | | |

Source: World Bank, *African Development Indicators* database.

duced convergence criteria, but it is unclear how these criteria would be used to decide whether countries were ready to proceed to monetary union.

## Tying the Hands of the Monetary Authorities

An important theme in discussions of monetary union, as well as in the literature on exchange rate arrangements, is that monetary policy flexibility often is not well used. For instance, Hausman and others (1999) argue that flexibility of exchange rates in Latin America has served no useful purpose because monetary authorities have succumbed to the temptation of overexpansionary policies leading to recurrent devaluations. As a result, countries with flexible rates pay a risk premium and they would benefit by simply giving up flexibility of the exchange rate (however, this is a view that is contested by others). Thus, Hausman and others argue for "dollarization," the replacement of the national currency by a stable international currency.

Why are the advantages of exchange rate and monetary policy flexibility not always obtained? Na-

# VI THE BENEFITS AND COSTS OF A COMMON CURRENCY FOR WEST AFRICA

tional central banks often are not independent of fiscal authorities that are myopic and concerned primarily with financing their expenditures. In the absence of other sources of financing, they may turn to the central bank; higher than desirable inflation frequently results. Even independent central banks may face incentives to create excessive inflation. At a general level, Barro and Gordon (1983) stress the value of "tying the hands" of the monetary authorities. According to their arguments, if a central bank uses expansionary monetary policy to attempt to correct a distortion in the economy causing excessive unemployment, but the private sector correctly anticipates the central bank's actions, unemployment would fail to improve while inflation would rise.

Monetary union, by creating supranational institutions, may in principle provide a constraint on central banks ("tying their hands"), making it easier for the monetary authorities to resist pressures to finance any particular government's fiscal deficit. Going in the other direction, however, monetary union may also encourage governments to allow fiscal positions to get out of hand—either with the expectation that they will be bailed out, or because the costs (in terms of higher interest rates, an overappreciated exchange rate, etc.) will be shared by other countries in the union, and not internalized in the high-deficit country. The experience of WAEMU showed that monetary union alone was not sufficient to lead to fiscal discipline (see Appendix II). Consistent with this potential problem, the EU has imposed strict rules to prevent monetary financing or bailouts of governments and an elaborate procedure to prevent excessive government deficits. Thus, tying the hands of the monetary authorities is not enough—one must also tie the hands of the fiscal authorities. Monetary union involves a major commitment, which only makes sense if the countries concerned are committed to a major transfer of sovereignty and a willingness to support supranational institutions.

Guillaume and Stasavage (2000) consider in some detail the experience in Africa with the use of monetary unions as a form of commitment to financial stability. They argue that monetary unions can effectively provide that commitment, but only if they satisfy three conditions: (1) exit from the union must be made costly by the loss of other benefits of regional integration or of assistance from industrial countries; (2) governance structures must be designed to enforce monetary rules; and (3) attempts by one country to break the rules of the union must be actively opposed by other governments in the union.

What practical steps does this imply for ECOWAS? First, making national central banks more independent is important, since they will continue to exist and have some influence (at least for a transition period) on monetary policy. Second, a monetary union is likely to be more successful and durable if accompanied by parallel linkages and agreements that make exit costly. Third, a stable monetary union requires both carefully drafted formal rules on monetary financing as well as the experience of mutual surveillance and the effective exercise of peer pressure to ensure de facto monetary and fiscal discipline.

## Convergence Criteria

Following the example of the EU and WAEMU, the non-WAEMU countries have set various targets for convergence. By end-2000 (end-2003), countries are expected to lower inflation to 10 percent (3 percent); raise gross official reserves to at least three months (six months) of imports; reduce central bank advances to no more than 10 percent of the previous year's tax revenues by end-2003; and cut the overall fiscal deficit (excluding grants) to no more than 5 percent (4 percent) of GDP. Exchange rate stability is to be added to the list of criteria, but it has not yet been defined precisely. Table 2.2 on page 5 presents the latest data for the existing convergence criteria.

ECOWAS countries currently are very far from achieving all the criteria. Ghana and Sierra Leone are experiencing very high inflation, as well as large fiscal deficits that are well over the target (Nigeria also has a large deficit). Four of the six (all except The Gambia and Nigeria) would not currently satisfy the relatively loose reserve target of three months of imports for 2000 (much less the criterion of twice that for 2003). Moreover, it should be recognized that achievement of exchange rate stability may lead to a rundown of reserves by some countries. Central bank advances as a percent of tax revenues are currently a multiple of the ceiling in all countries except Liberia and Ghana.

For comparison's sake, Table 2.3 on page 6 presents the position of WAEMU countries with respect to the convergence criteria agreed to by the countries of that region. Except for Guinea-Bissau, Niger, and Togo, WAEMU countries are much closer to achieving their convergence criteria, which are more stringent than those for ECOWAS as a whole.

The starting point for the countries of the proposed "second monetary union" is also much farther from convergence than was the case for most countries in the EU, where the transition period took about seven years from the signing of the Maastricht Treaty on European Union in February 1992.[21]

---

[21]Dating the start of the convergence process in the European Union is difficult, given that some of the stages (e.g., removal of capital controls by 1990) antedated signing of the Treaty, and the creation of the European Monetary System in 1979 was intended as stage I of a transition to monetary union. Formal convergence programs were first introduced in 1992.

Some of the EU conditions required achievement over several years, not just on the basis of one year's performance.[22] Moreover, many of the European countries had a long period of sound finances and low inflation. Nevertheless, qualification for monetary union was subject to intense scrutiny and efforts to harmonize data and close loopholes that might permit a temporary or unsustainable achievement of the criteria. For ECOWAS, it will be important to remove any ambiguity in defining convergence criteria, to ensure that they are calculated in the same way in all countries, and for countries proceeding to monetary union to have demonstrated their ability to meet the criteria in a sustained and durable fashion.

## Can a Common Currency Stimulate Other Forms of Integration?

A reputed advantage of monetary union is that it can stimulate other forms of integration. This point was debated extensively in the context of European integration between the "monetarists" (who argued in the affirmative) and the "economists" (who argued that monetary union must follow, not precede, other forms of integration). Whatever the merits of the argument, the views of the "economists" prevailed in the design of European Economic and Monetary Union.

As discussed in Appendix III, it seems that the evidence of a positive impact of monetary union on other aspects of integration is at best mixed. The comparison of WAEMU and CAEMC is instructive, since both have evolved from monetary unions formed at the same time, and both have the same external peg. Trade among the countries of the former is much greater than among the latter. WAEMU has achieved some success in harmonizing policies and in instituting surveillance; CAEMC has achieved much less. It seems likely that, by itself, a monetary union among disparate countries will not produce the other integration benefits. The objective of monetary union, however, could be a positive force if it initiates a sustained economic convergence process and involves building the basis for regional cooperation. The risk is that an ill-planned and premature monetary union might fail and endanger progress in other areas. If countries are not tied together in other ways, so that leaving the monetary union would mean losing other benefits (access to regional grants, for instance), the monetary union is unlikely to be durable.

---

[22]In particular, exchange rate stability was required for two years, though the widening of the bands of fluctuation made this condition less constraining from August 1993. The general government debt criterion also stipulated that the trend was important, not just the level at a particular point in time.

# VII  Options for Implementing Monetary Union in West Africa

In April 2000, the leaders of the six non-WAEMU ECOWAS countries agreed to form a "second monetary union" by 2003, which would then be merged with WAEMU in 2004. Preparations are under way to monitor the economic convergence of these countries in areas that are deemed important for monetary union. Each of the six non-WAEMU countries has agreed to set up a macroeconomic coordinating committee to speed the process.[23]

Given the importance of the undertaking, the steps leading to monetary union and its ultimate form need to be considered carefully. This chapter lays out some of the design and transition options and provides some tentative suggestions on the best strategies for implementing monetary union.

## The "Second Monetary Union"

### Design Issues

Fundamental choices must be made in designing a monetary union: whether (or when) to create a new currency or use an existing currency; what supranational institutions would be needed to ensure a single monetary and exchange rate policy; and what anchor would be provided for monetary policy—an external peg or an internal nominal target (e.g., targets for inflation, or for a money or credit aggregate)? The ultimate intention to merge the two unions should influence the design of the non-WAEMU monetary union; in particular, it only makes sense to invest heavily in the construction of new institutions if they are intended to be durable, rather than to be replaced when the broader union is established.

There would seem to be two major options for the non-WAEMU monetary union. In the first scenario, the non-WAEMU countries gradually would bring about convergence of their economies; this (perhaps accompanied by formal bands) would help to achieve exchange rate stability among their currencies, which would continue in existence and would not be irrevocably pegged. There would be no supranational central bank; instead, countries would interact through the ECOWAS Convergence Council to implement mutual surveillance over each others' policies. Each country would retain its central bank and monetary autonomy, and its success in achieving monetary convergence would be judged by reference to the rate of inflation and the degree of monetary stability. The result would be what Corden (1972) terms a "pseudo exchange rate union"—since there would be neither an irrevocable fixing of exchange rates nor a single monetary policy—or an "informal exchange rate union" (Cobham and Robson, 1994). This scenario would be appropriate if full monetary union among the non-WAEMU countries was not judged desirable, either because it would be superseded immediately by full monetary union with WAEMU or because the preconditions for the second monetary union among a sufficient number of countries were judged as not met.

The second scenario would involve the creation of a true monetary union for the non-WAEMU countries. The institutions of the second monetary union would be intended to be durable either because they would provide the nucleus for the subsequent merger with WAEMU, or because the ultimate goal of a merger of the two zones would not be viewed as imminent, so that the two zones would coexist for an extended period of time. In this scenario, the first step would be to achieve convergence of macro policies. Next, it would be necessary to create a new supranational central bank benefiting from the public support of member governments and with statutes that clearly established its independence. Then, given the importance of making a credible commitment to irrevocable parities, national currencies would be eliminated and replaced by a new single currency.[24]

The two scenarios differ considerably with respect to the time and effort needed for their achievement.

---

[23]"ECOWAS Single Currency Kicks Off," *This Day* (Lagos), July 17, 2000.

[24]For reasons discussed above, none of the existing central banks or national currencies seems to have the needed track record of stability, making the creation of a new central bank and currency desirable should this scenario be implemented.

The first scenario resembles the strategy employed in the European Monetary System. At one time, it seemed feasible to achieve European Economic and Monetary Union by a gradual narrowing of the margins of fluctuation around the exchange rate mechanism (ERM) central parities. Once those margins were virtually zero, then one of the main objectives of monetary union, namely exchange rate stability, would have been achieved, and it would then be a relatively simple matter to replace national currencies by the single European currency. Since the ERM was anchored by the deutsche mark and the strong and credible commitment of Germany's Bundesbank to price stability, not only the stability of the currencies among themselves, but also the stability of purchasing power of the common currency, would be assured. The ERM crises of 1992–93 destroyed this vision of monetary union in the EU. However, the speculative attacks against central parities were abetted by the removal of capital controls and the resulting high capital mobility.

ECOWAS would not face the same overwhelming weight of short-term capital flows; in any case, it could benefit from the ERM experience by not making exaggerated commitments to defend central parities that were out of line with fundamentals. By allowing flexibility in adjusting parities to large terms of trade shocks while requiring monetary authorities to stabilize their currencies in normal times, such a system could provide a zone of monetary stability without excessive rigidity and could be put in place within the planned timetable.

The second scenario resembles the institution building that was embodied in the Maastricht Treaty on European Union and implemented in the course of the 1990s in Europe. It is a difficult and time consuming process. In the EU, it was facilitated by public support for price stability, the strong political support for European integration, and the experience with functioning European institutions (including the earlier experience with monetary cooperation in the European Monetary System). As noted above, despite a relatively favorable starting point of macroeconomic convergence, the EU devoted much attention to designing a European Central Bank that would be insulated from political forces and to preparing surveillance procedures to limit fiscal deficits. It seems safe to say that the time and effort that would be needed for ECOWAS to design such institutions and make them work would be at least as great as the time and effort that was required for the EU, suggesting that this second scenario would not be possible within the horizon of 2003.

When considering monetary integration in Africa, Cobham and Robson (1994) argue that higher forms of integration constituted by full monetary union have all the benefits of lower forms (i.e., informal exchange rate unions) but fewer costs. This overstates the advantages of "tying the hands" of the monetary authorities, however.[25] Retaining the ability to modify parities until it is clear that convergence of economic structures and performance has been achieved is good insurance. Thus, an informal exchange rate union, with separate currencies that are stable within margins, may well be a preferable medium-term objective.

The choice between the first and second scenarios (or some hybrid) should also depend very much on the role that WAEMU, and its central bank, the Banque Central des Etats de l'Afrique de l'Ouest (BCEAO), would play in the combined monetary union. With a functioning supranational central bank and a currency that has delivered price stability for most of five decades, WAEMU has the requisite track record and reputation to provide the nucleus of the larger monetary union. However, neighboring countries have reservations about the CFA franc because it is viewed as a relic of French colonialism.[26] The French Treasury assures the currency's convertibility and it has been pegged (with one change in parity) continuously to the French franc for more than half a century. Although the creation of the euro has assured exchange rate stability vis-à-vis a much wider set of European countries, the relationship with France remains. France has representatives on the boards of the central banks of the two CFA zones and thus retains some influence over monetary policy decisions.

A more fundamental criticism of the arrangement is that it has stifled the development of African financial markets, channeled transactions through France, and perpetuated dependence on decisions taken in Europe (Monga and Tchatchouang, 1996). Although the advantages and disadvantages of a link to the euro are discussed below, if WAEMU provides the nucleus for the ECOWAS monetary union, it seems likely that the link with the French Treasury would have to be abandoned. In any case, a decision of the European Council on November 23, 1998, requires that France must submit for the Council's approval any change in the nature or scope of its exchange rate agreements with the CFA franc zone. Neither France nor its EU partners are likely to endorse an expansion of the French Treasury's guarantee to a much wider set of countries.[27] It is also unlikely that EU institutions would replace the French Treasury as a guarantor of convertibility. Any exchange rate link with an external currency would

---

[25]See also the discussion of the decline in influence of the "credibility hypothesis" in Tavlas (2000).
[26]See Asante and Abankwa (1999).
[27]For a discussion of the new status of the CFA zone, see Gnassou (1999).

# VII OPTIONS FOR IMPLEMENTING MONETARY UNION IN WEST AFRICA

then have to be assured by the central bank's own intervention and monetary policy settings, rather than by a European guarantee.

### Transition Issues

As suggested above, the design of the monetary union should influence the transition process. Several issues take on considerable importance: (1) the time allowed for transition to monetary union; (2) whether and how the convergence criteria are to be used to select the countries ready to go to monetary union at some point; and (3) the role of the exchange rate in the transition.

Choosing the second scenario means that institutions would have to be designed and created before monetary union could begin. The transition process would necessarily have to be longer, because the non-WAEMU monetary union would be considerably tighter in this case. Indeed, the negotiation of a treaty setting up a new central bank, if the latter is to have its powers, instruments, and responsibilities spelled out, would require decisions on numerous technical details, as well as the resolution of political disagreements that could arise on such things as the location of the bank, the number and country of origin of its governing board members, the pooling of foreign exchange reserves, and the allocation of seigniorage.

The first scenario of a looser monetary union, retaining existing institutions, could begin earlier, perhaps without a firm decision as to the ultimate destination or how to get there. Other issues could be faced later—for instance, at a second stage when the merger with WAEMU was contemplated. Thus, in principle, an informal monetary union could exist by 2003—but that would depend on the degree of commitment of national policymakers to macroeconomic convergence.

The use of convergence criteria as qualifiers for entry to monetary union would also differ in the two cases. In the first scenario, a sharp distinction between those "in" monetary union and the "outs" would not be necessary. Instead, countries would be more or less able to meet the criteria and, among other benefits of macroeconomic stability, this would mean that their currencies would be more or less fixed in terms of some reference currency (discussed below). It would be in each country's interest to meet the convergence criteria, but not doing so would not trigger exclusion from monetary union at this stage or produce strong externalities on other countries, as would be the case for a full monetary union. In the second scenario, however, it would be very important for the credibility and durability of the monetary union for countries to have demonstrated their ability to limit monetary financing, achieve low inflation, and limit their budgetary deficits. Admitting a non-convergent country would cause problems both for the country concerned (since it would not have the structures to support the monetary discipline of the union's policies) and for the union as a whole (especially if the country were a large country, because it could derail the union's monetary policy).

The exchange rate could be given a role in the convergence process, as in the transition to European Economic and Monetary Union. Achievement of a degree of exchange rate stability, somehow defined, could either be a condition for entry into the non-WAEMU monetary union (scenario two) or into the ultimate ECOWAS monetary union. The question of a reference currency then arises. The European Monetary System created a parity grid and a basket currency (the European Currency Unit, ECU) so that the system was in principle symmetric. In practice, the system revolved around the deutsche mark, which provided the anchor given the strong anti-inflation credibility of the German Bundesbank and the strength of the German economy. In non-WAEMU ECOWAS, no currency plays a similar role nor does it seem useful to create a currency composite, with its technical difficulties. Instead, if an exchange rate stability criterion is desired, then the exchange rate against the euro or an existing basket currency like the special drawing right (SDR) would be a natural reference rate.[28] Macroeconomic convergence between WAEMU and non-WAEMU countries would be facilitated by the choice of the euro, since the CFA franc is pegged to the euro. Exchange rate stability against the euro would then imply exchange rate stability among the countries of the region. This is consistent with the recommendation of Cobham and Robson (1994, p. 292):

> "For countries that are not committed to the goal of monetary integration, but are interested in moving at least some way toward it, two policies can be suggested: first, they should peg their currencies to the same external anchor; and secondly they should make current and capital account transactions convertible."

However, a firm peg to the euro would be exposed to fluctuations of the exchange rate between the U.S. dollar and the euro; in that regard, an SDR peg would be preferable.

---

[28]The Dakar meeting of ECOWAS central bank governors in May 2000 endorsed the West African Unit of Account, which is linked one-for-one to the SDR, as the numeraire for evaluating exchange rate stability. However, it appears that this issue has not been definitively resolved and will be the subject of a study by the "interim institution," to be created shortly.

## The Second Stage: Full Monetary Union in ECOWAS

Assuming that a full monetary union is achieved, extending across both WAEMU and at least some non-WAEMU countries, the fundamental question to address is the choice of an anchor for monetary policy. The principal alternatives are an exchange rate peg and a target for domestic inflation or a monetary aggregate (accompanied by a flexible exchange rate, albeit with some central bank intervention in the foreign exchange market for smoothing purposes).

The literature on fixed versus flexible exchange rates, reviewed above, is relevant for the choice for the ECOWAS union. Although members of ECOWAS conduct about 10 percent of their international trade within the union, more than 40 percent of ECOWAS trade is with countries of the EU. Thus, a euro peg would provide exchange rate stability with regard to more than 50 percent of member countries' international trade.

Nevertheless, the commodity composition of ECOWAS exports is, and would continue to be, very different from that of the EU. As a result, the terms of trade would continue to vary considerably and a drop in the world price of ECOWAS exports of oil, cocoa, etc. would have a depressing effect on the region's equilibrium real exchange rate. If the exchange rate against the euro could not change, this might have deflationary consequences—as occurred in WAEMU in the 1986–93 period. Moreover, if the exchange rate of the euro against the U.S. dollar varied, this would also affect the competitiveness of ECOWAS exports. This latter problem could be addressed by pegging the currency to a basket composed of the euro and the U.S. dollar, with the former being given a larger weight, reflecting the relative importance of European and U.S. trade. Alternatively, the currency could be pegged to the SDR, which includes the dollar, euro, yen, and pound sterling.

An SDR peg would have the advantage of linking to other aspects of the ECOWAS integration process (i.e., the West African Unit of Account) and would distinguish the ECOWAS monetary union from WAEMU, with its peg to the euro. However, an SDR peg would be less immediately relevant to actual trade and capital transactions since it would not involve an existing national currency. It might, as a result, involve greater transactions costs and a less visible anchor for monetary policy.

There are three additional objections to an exchange rate peg, however. First, inadequate flexibility of the peg will at times lead to large overvaluations, since it will be difficult to match consistently the low inflation of the industrial countries. This has been the experience in much of sub-Saharan Africa (and other developing regions) and has contributed to a move away from pegged exchange rates. Second, adjustable pegs are inherently unstable because they do not involve a credible commitment to a fixed rate, so that in the presence of some degree of capital mobility they are subject to speculative attacks. Although the scope for capital movements in ECOWAS is presently restricted, this could become a factor with the passage of time. Finally, developing country exchange rate pegs that do not benefit from an external guarantee or a transparent institutional setup like a currency board have often been associated with multiple currency practices and the non-market allocation of foreign exchange at the official rate, with the scope that this allows for corruption and inefficiency.

The alternative of a domestic nominal anchor is more demanding, in that it requires establishing a credible and effective operating procedure for delivering monetary stability; in practice, sub-Saharan African countries have found this difficult to do. As already noted, non-WAEMU ECOWAS countries have experienced high and variable inflation. The choice of a domestic nominal anchor is likely to be between a monetary aggregate and inflation. In a number of countries, monetary aggregate targets have suffered from the instability of money demand. Regarding inflation targeting, there are several prerequisites for its effective implementation—in addition to monetary independence for the central bank, which is necessary for any effective monetary policy. These prerequisites include a quantified relationship between monetary instruments and inflation in 12–18 months, given the lags involved (see Masson, Savastano, and Sharma, 1997). Such a relationship may be difficult to establish in developing countries with administered prices and where inflation data are poor given the size of the informal sector. Another requirement for the success of the policy is a public consensus in favor of low inflation and support for economic policy based on it—a condition that is not necessarily present in ECOWAS countries. In sum, neither policy unequivocally dominates the other: an independent monetary policy would have the benefits of flexibility but would be demanding in terms of institutions and discipline, while a firmly pegged rate would be more rigid but would have the advantages of transparency and stability.

# VIII Conclusions: The Perspective of Regional Integration

Plans for monetary union among ECOWAS countries are driven by a strong desire to increase regional economic linkages and political solidarity. Since many countries in the region are small both in terms of population and GDP, regional integration is seen as a way of increasing economic clout and bargaining power on the global scene. Larger markets may allow economies of scale and gains from trade to be exploited and increase production efficiency. Monetary union may provide a visible symbol of the commitment to regional integration—over and above its purely economic benefits that derive from greater economic efficiency and lower transactions costs.

It is important to recognize, however, that currency union is neither necessary nor sufficient for the growth of regional trade—as evidenced by the strong ties among the North American Free Trade Agreement (NAFTA) countries, on the one hand, and the relatively low integration among WAEMU and especially CAEMC countries after 50 years of monetary union, on the other. Although there is some evidence that monetary union can expand trade and thus boost growth, it will be more crucial for growth for each ECOWAS country to "put its own house in order"—that is, put in place the appropriate macroeconomic discipline and structural policies.

In addition, the potential benefits of monetary union must be weighed against potential costs. A single monetary and exchange rate policy will not allow countries to make different adjustments when they face asymmetric terms of trade (and other) shocks. In particular, the necessary adjustment policies for Nigeria, an oil exporter, are likely to be opposite those for the oil importing countries of ECOWAS in the face of a change in the price of oil. In general, inadequate flexibility of exchange rate pegs can lead to large overvaluations, while adjustable pegs have a degree of inherent instability and lack of credibility. The non-WAEMU countries' history with exchange rate pegs involved inefficiency and corruption associated with non-market allocation of foreign exchange at the official rate—a past that should not be repeated. Finally, while monetary union could aid as an "agency of restraint" promoting fiscal discipline, perversely, it could also encourage governments to allow fiscal positions to get out of hand.

Moreover, the institution building required to create a successful monetary union has costs—especially if it duplicates existing national bureaucracies—and takes time. The push for monetary integration must not be allowed to distract attention from more fundamental problems or to divert resources away from where they are most needed. Indeed, without fiscal discipline accompanied by wage/price flexibility and factor mobility in the economy, a currency union would not have the desired benefits and might not be sustainable.

Regional integration resulting in greater trade among ECOWAS countries may help increase efficiency of production. Trade among developing countries, in general, is likely to have fewer efficiency benefits than trade with developed countries, however, because the possibilities of exploiting complementarities are less. North-South trade opens the door to technology transfers necessary for development. In implementing regional integration, therefore, one must avoid the risks of trade diversion away from multilateral trade and toward intraregional trade. Regional integration should be seen as a steppingstone to the benefits of wider trade liberalization, rather than a way to increase protection of regional "infant industries."

The design of a new central bank must be done carefully and this will require solving numerous technical and political problems. Regional surveillance must be made effective in limiting excessive deficits and in imposing sanctions against countries that violate the rules of the union. As in the EU, it will be important to prove that countries are ready and fully committed to proceed to monetary union, before rushing into it. A strong sense of regional solidarity will be an essential ingredient for getting through periods of stress.

Whether the institutional preparation for a non-WAEMU monetary union is justified by the expected benefits depends in part on how long this monetary union is expected to last, before being re-

## Conclusions: The Perspective of Regional Integration

placed by a full ECOWAS monetary union. In the meantime, exchange rate stability could be achieved instead by limiting fluctuations among the currencies of member countries or by a common peg to the euro or a basket of currencies, without creation of a full monetary union, while the "agency of restraint" could, in principle, be achieved by setting up other regional institutions that provide mutual surveillance and peer pressure. The creation of a looser form of monetary cooperation would be less costly, could be achieved sooner, and would allow some flexibility in response to asymmetric shocks.

Attempting a hasty and ill-prepared monetary union, instead of helping the cause of regional integration, could set it back if monetary union proved not to be a success. Two eventualities in particular need to be avoided. In one case, a new money is introduced but the regional central bank is unable to resist pressures for monetization. As a result, the new currency is associated with continued exchange rate depreciation against major international currencies and high inflation, producing a currency that no one wants to hold. For countries currently benefiting from monetary stability, this would be a step backward, tending to discredit the regional integration project. Investing in the institutional guarantees of central bank independence and sound fiscal policies would avoid this outcome. The second problematic case might involve a regional central bank that was successful in implementing financial discipline, but where some member countries asked to leave the monetary union on finding that they could not accept the constraints on monetary financing and export competitiveness. This would be less likely to occur in a case where monetary union members had already adapted to the constraints through an extended period of satisfying convergence criteria and they were benefiting from other aspects of regional integration which might be lost following withdrawal from monetary union. In either case of breakdown of the monetary union, regional solidarity and economic performance would have been harmed, not helped, by the monetary union.

The foregoing considerations suggest that the momentum in favor of monetary union should be channeled into the crucial first phase of enhanced mutual surveillance and emphasis on each country improving its macroeconomic and structural policies. Success in this endeavor would in and of itself help to increase exchange rate stability. In addition, there could be a coordinated attempt to narrow the fluctuation ranges of regional currencies, without creating a formal monetary union among non-WAEMU countries. At this point, a full ECOWAS monetary union, including both WAEMU and non-WAEMU countries, could be envisioned, and preparations begun. Given the expected time to achieve convergence and to design the necessary institutions, it seems doubtful that the ECOWAS monetary union planned for 2004 is feasible. Instead, it should await much fuller economic convergence and reinforced political solidarity within the region.

# Appendix I   Economic Policies in Non-WAEMU Countries

## Nigeria

Nigeria has had generally weak economic performance resulting from economic mismanagement, fiscal indiscipline, unproductive public spending, persistent exchange rate overvaluation, and over regulation. Structural reforms during 1986–90 resulted in substantial growth, but policy weakenings and reversals afterward brought about stagflation. Nigerians became convinced that structural adjustment was responsible for all their country's economic ills, including the depreciating naira, high and variable inflation, and the collapse of domestic industry (Moser and others, 1997). In 1994 the government reimposed interest rate controls and eliminated the free market for foreign exchange, pegging the currency at an overvalued rate. Partial deregulation began again in 1995, with the liberalization of exchange rate controls, restoration of foreign exchange bureaus, and introduction of a dual exchange rate regime, with an administratively determined official rate and a flexible auction rate. Relatively prudent fiscal and monetary policies during 1996–97 together with high oil prices helped reduce inflation from a peak of 77 percent in 1994 to 10 percent in 1997, and increase average real GDP growth to 4 percent. Economic growth, however, continued to be hampered by fuel, power, and fertilizer shortages, and political uncertainties.

By early 1998, Nigeria had a multiple exchange rate system: an artificially overvalued official rate for government and oil transactions, an "autonomous foreign exchange market" (AFEM) with a rate administratively determined in a managed float (with reference to the interbank and parallel rate, and supported by net infusions of foreign exchange from oil exports), plus foreign exchange bureaus and an active parallel market. Access to foreign exchange for current account transactions was quite liberal, although some restrictions remained.

The Abubakhar administration abolished the official exchange rate in 1998. Some initial progress in controlling government spending was made in the face of sharp drops in petroleum revenues, but the budget deficit increased to over 8 percent in the first half of 1999, financed by central bank credit. Real change began in June 1999, as democratically elected President Olusegun Obasanjo took office, taking immediate actions to combat corruption and build public confidence. Inflation fell and the exchange rate stabilized. There have been no signs of a sustained revival in real GDP growth, however. The abolition of the AFEM and the enhancement of the interbank (or IFEM) market has led to a more flexible, market-determined exchange rate for the naira. In the program for 2000/01 supported by an IMF Stand-By Arrangement, the Nigerian authorities have made a commitment to sustained macroeconomic stability and exchange rate flexibility.

## Ghana

By 1983, triple-digit inflation and parallel market premiums, sharply negative growth, and a good portion of economic activity occurring outside legal channels brought Ghana's economy to the brink of collapse. The Economic Recovery Program (ERP) of 1983–91 began with an effective 800 percent devaluation of the nominal exchange rate and very gradually liberalized the exchange and trade system by introducing foreign exchange auctions and the licensing of foreign exchange bureaus. The real exchange rate depreciated throughout the period, correcting overvaluation and responding appropriately to declines in the terms of trade. Substantial progress was made in controlling fiscal and monetary policies, although inflation remained quite variable. Although stabilization successes were impressive, real economic growth recovered to an average of only 2 percent during this period, related to the weak private investment response to the reforms. Loss of fiscal control began again in 1992, as large civil service wage increases associated with the elections rekindled inflationary expectations. Inflation reached 70 percent in 1995 (1996 was another election year), but it decelerated to 14 percent by end-1999. However, rapid cedi depreciation in late 1999 and 2000 brought inflationary pressures back to the 30 percent level.

The real exchange rate has been appreciating since 1995, eroding Ghana's competitiveness relative to Côte d'Ivoire, its CFA neighbor and fellow cocoa exporter. By 1999, there was a concern that the increasing appreciation would negatively affect the strong growth in nontraditional exports. The real depreciation during 2000, however, has returned the currency to the most competitive level over the last decade.

The process of broadening access and improving the efficiency of the exchange market continued under the Economic Recovery Program, taking another step forward in 1992 with the replacement of the foreign exchange auction with an interbank market. Currently, however, the market is still experiencing operating problems, as it is actually a market between the central bank and the commercial banks, rather than a true interbank market.

Following some improvement in fiscal control in 1998, Ghana suffered a major terms of trade shock in 1999, as world prices for its main exports (cocoa and gold) plummeted and oil prices doubled. Neither fiscal nor monetary policies responded appropriately, however. The government maintained too high a cocoa price for farmers that severely compromised revenue from cocoa taxes and borrowed from the banking system to fill the resulting higher deficit. Fearing that rapid depreciation would further stoke inflation, the Bank of Ghana (central bank) intervened in the foreign exchange market to slow nominal depreciation. This strategy was finally forced to end by November 1999, when reserves were run down to dangerously low levels.

## The Gambia

Economic activity in The Gambia began declining in the late 1970s. The exchange rate, pegged to the pound sterling, became increasingly overvalued. Oil price shocks, low world market prices for groundnuts, and a long drought in the Sahel contributed to the economic decline as did excessive domestic borrowing and money creation to finance the fiscal deficit. The overvalued currency discouraged the surrender of export proceeds to the official banking system, inducing a growing external indebtedness and depletion of gross official reserves. In addition, external payment arrears and a large parallel market emerged.

The centerpiece of the Economic Recovery Program (ERP) beginning in 1986 was the flotation of the Gambian currency (dalasi), resulting in a nominal depreciation of approximately 78 percent and the removal of restrictions on foreign exchange transactions. Government policy reforms in other areas supported the exchange market reforms: liberalization of controls on prices and interest rates, and large reductions in the budget deficit. A large inflow of foreign aid is also credited as having helped stabilize the exchange rate. The reform has been judged as an example of quite rapid stabilization due to a combination of good policies, luck (end of drought), and aid (Radelet, 1993; McPherson and Radelet, 1991).

Following the large real depreciation in 1986, there was some appreciation of the real exchange rate until 1990.

The 1994 coup led to a sharp drop in aid, and a reduction in tourism receipts and problems for the re-export trade—both increasingly important sectors of the economy. The Gambia's loss of competitiveness with Senegal after the 1994 CFA devaluation (and the imposition of border controls by Senegal until 1996) also hurt re-export trade. Output declined by 3.4 percent in 1994–95. After picking up in 1995–96, economic performance deteriorated again in 1996–97, a period of transition from military to civilian rule, as the government made inappropriate policy responses to adverse shocks—primarily through an overly expansionary fiscal stance. The economy began to improve in 1998, although substantial governance problems occurred in 1999 as the government seized the Gambia Groundnut Corporation, incurred excessive debt, and engaged in suspicious extrabudgetary spending. Still, the budget deficit was brought down from 12 percent in 1995–96 to 4.8 percent in 1998–99, and inflation remained relatively low.

The market-based flexible exchange rate is viewed as having served the economy well. There has been no major deterioration in competitiveness since 1990 based on the real exchange rate, although the 1994 CFA devaluation improved Senegal and Mali's relative competitiveness. Government intervention in the foreign exchange market has been limited to smoothing exchange rate fluctuations and minimizing reserve losses. However, the existence of a 10 percent spread between the parallel and interbank market reveals limited competition in the interbank market and the need for its further development.

## Guinea

Until 1984, Guinea had a centrally planned, command economy system, with nearly the entire formal sector controlled by a large, inefficient public sector sustained by royalties of foreign-owned bauxite companies. A comprehensive reform program, including liberalization of the foreign exchange system, made progress in transitioning to a market economy during 1985–95. GDP growth increased to an annual average of 4 percent. The fiscal position improved impressively given the cumulative decline in bauxite and alumina prices, which were the major source of government revenue.

From 1986–94, a managed float through an auction market determined the exchange rate. It has been judged as a successful exchange rate based stabilization (Azam and Diakité, 1999). The central bank adopted a relatively low rate of crawl, independent of the parallel rate, and inflation declined from 65 percent in 1986 to 4 percent in 1994. The credibility of the anti-inflation policy has been substantially credited to the strong personality of the governor of the central bank, Kerfalla Yansane. Together with a relatively tight domestic credit policy, this enabled the accumulation of foreign exchange reserves, used for exchange rate based stabilization, even against the background of deteriorating terms of trade.

The economy deteriorated somewhat in 1996, due to problems associated with a failed mutiny by the army. Broad macroeconomic equilibrium was maintained, however, and the overall budget deficit (including grants) was less than 3 percent. External developments created difficulties beginning in the second half of 1998 when the Asian crisis triggered a sharp fall in prices of bauxite and alumina; deteriorating security in neighboring countries Sierra Leone, Guinea-Bissau, and Liberia required the government to spend substantial amounts on peacekeeping troops; and uncertainty about stability surrounded the December 1998 elections. The government financed the deteriorating fiscal balance in 1999 by borrowing from the central bank.

From 1994–99, the exchange rate was determined in an interbank market, although in recent years the government has intervened excessively to keep the rate artificially high. Before September 1999, the foreign exchange market was highly segmented. State enterprises and donors, operating through two large banks, and large importers dominated an official market. Remaining transactions took place in a so-called parallel market of foreign exchange bureaus, which actually have official status. The spread between the two rates ranged from 4–6 percent until mid-1998, when the spread began widening and market segmentation became more pronounced, with "shortages" in the parallel market while those with access to official rates earned substantial rents. The central bank introduced a weekly auction for foreign exchange, which helped to reduce the spread significantly, and since end-1999 it has fluctuated between plus or minus 3 percent. The introduction of a foreign exchange auction also led to a depreciation of 26 percent in the last four months of 1999, but since then the official rate has appreciated.

## Cape Verde

From 1975–91, Cape Verde pursued an inward-oriented, activist development strategy based on central planning and an economically dominant public sector. Still, relatively prudent policies (and large foreign transfers) allowed economic growth to proceed at a solid pace through the 1980s. By the late 1980s, aid and remittances began declining. Rather than cutting large expenditures, the government used bank credit to finance deficits. Unemployment and inflation rose, and official reserves fell. Movement toward a more market-oriented economy began in 1992, with an adjustment program adopted by a new government under a new constitution. The reforms restored reasonable growth, with significant contributions from services and foreign investment in export-oriented manufacturing. Until 1997, however, fiscal policies were unsustainably lax, leading to accumulation of domestic debt and depletion of foreign exchange reserves to levels covering as little as one-half month's worth of imports in 1996.

Cape Verde began a precautionary arrangement with the IMF in 1998, with the objectives of reducing fiscal imbalances, privatizing, lowering domestic debt, and liberalizing the trade and exchange rate system. Rapid progress followed: real GDP growth increased to 8 percent in 1998–99 and inflation was halved from 8.6 percent in 1997 to 4.3 percent in 1999. Current account and capital transactions were liberalized in mid-1998, policies aimed at ensuring the convertibility of the Cape Verde escudo. In order to signal a commitment to low inflation and macroeconomic stability, the basket peg was replaced with a fixed link of the Cape Verde escudo to the Portuguese escudo and, since 1999, a peg to the EU's common currency, the euro.

Spending overruns worsened the fiscal situation in the second half of 1999. Given the currency peg, this immediately put pressure on international reserves. The authorities responded inappropriately by temporarily introducing foreign exchange rationing. The fiscal overruns were partially financed by credit from the central bank and also from a credit line facility with Portugal. The periods of fiscal deterioration—and their impact on prices, reserves, and investor confidence—show up clearly in appreciations of the real exchange rate in 1997 and the second half of 1998. Prior to this period, during the 1990s, the real exchange rate had been relatively stable.

## Liberia

Liberia's economic situation deteriorated in the 1980s following terms of trade declines, economic mismanagement, and mounting arrears that led to a breakdown of relations with creditors and donors. The 1989–97 civil war brought most economic activity to a virtual standstill. Following a peace agreement and democratic elections in 1997, the post-conflict recovery has been quite strong: real GDP doubled in 1997 and grew by 30 percent in 1998, bringing domestic production back to one-third of the pre-war level. This was largely due to recoveries in agriculture, forestry, and rubber, although not in the important iron ore sector.

The U.S. dollar is legal tender and the Liberian dollar was held at a fixed one-for-one parity until August 1998, when the rate became market determined. This change was made given the country's vulnerability to external shocks and lack of reserves. In March 2000 a new Liberian dollar replaced the Liberty and JJ Roberts notes. The exchange and trade system was liberalized in 1997–98, including an elimination of government monopolies on exporting of cash crops and elimination of foreign exchange surrender requirements on agricultural exports.

A new central bank was established in November 1999. For now, the central bank will not extend credit to the government and issuance of currency will be limited to exchange for the existing stock and the purchase of foreign currency to begin to rebuild international reserves. Thus, with a fixed stock of money and an illiquid central bank, monetary policy has had little scope. The exchange rate and inflation remained stable in 1998–99 in the context of a balanced fiscal position (cash basis) and fixed supply of currency. However, there was a substantial deterioration in the fiscal position during 1999 due to extrabudgetary expenditures, which has since been corrected.

## Sierra Leone

Sierra Leone's economic situation spiraled downward in the 1980s in the context of pervasive government control and intervention. Budget deficits (financed by money creation) averaged more than 12 percent, causing inflation to spiral and peak at 167 percent in 1986–87. The parallel market premium also reached triple digits, so that potential revenue from the mining sector was lost through smuggling and tax evasion, while the overvalued exchange rate and import subsidies led to smuggling of imports out to neighboring countries. An attempt at an adjustment program in 1986–87—which included an exchange rate float—failed.

A full-scale reform program began in 1989–90, with significant liberalization of the exchange and trade system, beginning in 1990, as the program's centerpiece. The parallel and official exchange rates were effectively unified through a float in an interbank market, with a large initial nominal depreciation. The real exchange rate, which exhibited massive fluctuations in the 1980s, depreciated with the liberalization of 1990 and since that point the size of changes has been substantially smaller. Overall results of the reform process were initially mixed as weak fiscal discipline contributed to monetary instability. By 1992, however, the successful exchange liberalization began to attract foreign assistance and the fiscal situation improved, leading to a buildup of reserves and a fall in inflation. It was still very difficult to register any improvements to growth during this period, however, as the economic infrastructure in mining and agricultural exports had nearly collapsed after years of neglect and rebel-related disruptions.

Rebel conflicts and civil war, during which rebels seized the rutile and bauxite mines that generated most export earnings and sizable parts of government revenues, caused the economic situation to deteriorate from 1992. Some gains in stabilization and economic recovery were achieved following the peace agreement and elections of 1996, but the country has subsequently been reengulfed by civil war.

# Appendix II   Existing and Failed Currency Unions

## Eastern Caribbean Currency Union

The ECCU consists of eight small island countries: Anguilla, Antigua and Barbuda, Dominica, Grenada, Montserrat, St. Kitts and Nevis, St. Lucia, and St. Vincent and the Grenadines.[1] Except for Anguilla and Montserrat, they are independent countries. Population ranges from 41,000 in St. Kitts and Nevis to 140,000 in St. Lucia (Randall, 1998). The countries have traditionally been primary commodity producers (banana, sugar, root crops), but tourism is now the most important source of foreign exchange earnings. Collectively, the GDP of the eight-member ECCU was $2.5 billion in 1998, with per capita income ranging from $2,700 in St Vincent and the Grenadines to $8,700 in Antigua and Barbuda.

The ECC Authority was formed in 1965 as the monetary authority for ECCU members and replaced in 1983 by the Eastern Caribbean Central Bank (ECCB). The Eastern Caribbean dollar (EC$) was initially pegged to the pound sterling. In 1976, the Eastern Caribbean dollar was pegged to the U.S. dollar at the then prevailing cross rate of EC$2.70/US$1, which remains in effect.

There is a single central bank for the monetary union and a single monetary policy. The ECCB operates as a quasi currency board, in which lending to member governments is strictly limited by statute and 60 percent of its monetary liabilities are required to be backed by foreign currency assets. In practice, the foreign exchange cover has been considerably higher, usually in excess of 95 percent in recent years. Foreign assets are part of a common pool and are not assigned to individual countries.

The main monetary policy objective is to maintain foreign exchange cover. The main policy tool is domestic credit expansion.

The ECCB has maintained a uniform reserve requirement of 6 percent since its inception, although it has the power to change it. In 1984, the ECCB established a facility for "bankers' fixed deposits" in U.S. dollars, which pay competitive rates.

There are 44 commercial banks operating in the area, of which six are "branch banks" of foreign banks that have continued since independence and that typically operate separately and independently in several countries of the region. The remaining 38 banks are locally incorporated and include government-owned, private, and locally incorporated branches of foreign banks. They are subject to minimum capital requirements, and in 1995 the regulations for loan loss provisioning were tightened.

There are restrictions on the flow of funds both within and outside the ECCB area. The current limit on purchases of foreign exchange for invisibles and capital transactions is EC$250,000, but all bona fide requests are honored. There is not a uniform regime with respect to the capital account, with each member applying some restrictions both with respect to transactions with other members and nonmembers, to varying degrees. Restrictions on capital flows have in the past impeded the creation of a single money market and contributed to the segmentation of the regional banking market and the persistence of large spreads between lending and deposit rates as well as differences in rates across countries (Randall, 1998).

Internal trade of the area is small. Although complete data are not available, a rough estimate suggests that less than 10 percent of ECCU members' total trade is accounted for by trade within the region (IMF, *Direction of Trade Statistics, 1999*).

## The Euro Area

The current members of the euro area are Austria, Belgium, Finland, France, Germany, Greece, Ireland, Italy, Luxembourg, the Netherlands, Portugal, and Spain. Other current and prospective European Union (EU) members are expected to join over the coming decade. At the formation of the euro area in 1999, the member countries accounted for 15.5 percent of world GDP and 32 percent of world exports (IMF 1999, Statistical Appendix Table A).

---

[1]See Van Beek and others (2000).

The euro area was formed after a long transition period and the prior creation of a customs union (1957) and a single market for goods and factors (1986). The Werner Report of 1970 recommended a monetary union among (then) European Community members by 1980. In 1979, the formation of the European Monetary System enhanced exchange rate cooperation, creating margins of fluctuation around fixed but adjustable central parities, and credit facilities for intervention. In 1989, the Delors Report gave fresh impetus to the regional integration project, leading to the signing of the Maastricht Treaty on European Union in February 1992. The absence of capital account restrictions (remaining ones had been removed by 1990) and uncertainty about ratification of the Treaty led to speculative attacks against a number of EMS currencies in the September 1992–July 1993 period, the withdrawal of the Italian lira and pound sterling from the exchange rate mechanism, several devaluations of other central parities, and the widening of the bands of fluctuation to plus or minus 15 percent at the beginning of August 1993.

Despite the fact that the EU consists of advanced countries that all have high per capita incomes, diversified economies, relatively low inflation, and a long history of cooperation, the Treaty mandated a long transition period in which countries had to prove that they had converged to low fiscal deficits, low inflation and interest rates, and exchange rate stability.

Monetary financing of governments is strictly prohibited by the Treaty. Moreover, the constraints on fiscal policy upon joining monetary union were further strengthened by agreement on the Stability and Growth Pact, which included provisions for assessing sanctions of up to half a percent of GDP on countries exceeding the deficit ceiling of 3 percent of GDP.

The euro is fully convertible on current and capital accounts.

Monetary policy is determined by the European Central Bank, on whose Governing Council each of the member countries is represented. There is a single monetary policy and set of official interest rates for the entire zone. Monetary policy is implemented in part by the national central banks; together, the ECB and national central banks make up the European System of Central Banks. Foreign exchange reserves are partly pooled and partly retained by national central banks.

The objective of monetary policy is to maintain price stability, and, subject to that objective being achieved, to support EU economic activity. Direct or indirect monetary financing of governments is prohibited. The main policy instrument is the interest rate on advances to commercial banks.

Monetary policy is built on two "pillars": targets for the growth of a monetary aggregate (M3) and for inflation. There is no target for the external value of the euro, which fluctuates against other major currencies.

Economic activity in the countries of the euro area is very integrated, with countries' production being relatively similar and very diversified. Internal trade within the region in 1998 was 46 percent of both imports and exports of member countries (IMF, *Direction of Trade Statistics, 1999*).

Other policies and institutions supporting regional integration in the EU include the common market, European Court of Justice, European Coal and Steel Community, Single European Act, Common Agricultural Policy, and extensive harmonization of regulations in a number of areas.

## The CFA Franc Zone in Africa

The CFA franc zone is composed of two zones of mainly Francophone countries in West and Central Africa. The West African CFA zone is the West African Economic and Monetary Union (WAEMU) or l'Union Economique et Monétaire Ouest Africaine (UEMOA), with its central bank, the Banque Centrale des Etats Ouest Africains (BCEAO). The Central African CFA zone is the Central African Economic and Monetary Community (CAEMC) or Communauté Economique et Monétaire de l'Afrique Centrale (CEMAC), with its central bank, the Banque des Etats de l'Afrique Centrale (BEAC). The WAEMU members are Benin, Burkina Faso, Côte d'Ivoire, Guinea-Bissau, Mali, Niger, Senegal, and Togo while Cameroon, Central African Republic, Chad, Congo, Equatorial Guinea, and Gabon are members of CAEMC.

Each regional grouping issues its own CFA franc, but they are exchangeable one-for-one against each other. The convertibility of the CFA franc at its parity against the French franc (100 CFAF=1 FF) is provided by the French Treasury through an Operations Account, where overdrafts are potentially unlimited. The CFA franc has been pegged to the euro since 1999 via its French franc peg. (The Comoros also pegs its currency, the Comorian franc, to the French franc and, since 1999, to the euro.) The current institutional arrangements for monetary policy in the CFA zone were established by treaties among members and France in 1972–73, but the CFA franc goes back to the second world war, when French colonies in Africa were grouped into two zones. The parity against the French franc remained constant from 1948 to 1994, when it was devalued from 50 CFA francs per French franc to 100 CFA francs.

For each of the two zones, member countries' reserves are held in separate Operations Accounts with the French Treasury. Each zone is required to hold external assets at least equal to 20 percent of the central bank's sight deposits. If that threshold is breached, the central bank needs to take extraordinary measures to correct the situation. The West African CFA zone was in deficit from 1980–84 and again from 1988–89, but the overall position in the operations account of the two zones together has only been in (small) deficit in 1983, 1987, and 1988. Since the 1994 devaluation, the positions of the two zones have been in substantial surplus.

The regional Council of Ministers and the central banks' Boards decide monetary targets, on the basis of submissions from national monetary authorities, subject to a limit on central bank financing of each government equal to 20 percent of the previous year's budgetary revenues. The central banks' main policy tool has been rediscount ceilings. However, bank credits for marketing, stockpiling, and crop exports were not included in the BEAC's rediscount ceilings, and in the 1980s and early 1990s this constituted a source of monetary expansion outside the central bank's control, especially to the largest CAEMC country, Cameroon. These credits were rediscounted automatically and at concessional rates (Nascimento, 1994). A similar situation existed in the West African zone, where the larger countries (Côte d'Ivoire and Senegal) avoided direct controls on financing by borrowing from commercial and development banks, which could obtain refinancing from the BCEAO at concessional rates. The lack of control over these credits opened the door to excessive lending to governments, despite respect of the formal ceilings on direct financing. As a result, existing rules did not achieve fiscal discipline (Stasavage, 1996). Excessive fiscal deficits developed in both zones, exacerbating overvaluation of the CFA franc related to terms of trade shocks and the appreciation of the French franc against the U.S. dollar in the 1987–93 period. Since prudential ratios on banks were not adequately enforced, a banking crisis occurred in both zones in this period and the central banks, which had extended loans to the banks, ended up the major creditors. In effect, the larger countries, which had benefited from the commercial bank loans, obtained seigniorage (Stasavage, 1996; Nascimento, 1994).

The overvaluation and general recession led to the crisis and devaluation of the CFA franc in January 1994.

Current account convertibility, although established in principle, is in fact subject to restriction. For instance, the repurchase by the central banks of their bank notes circulating outside the zone was suspended during the exchange rate crisis in July 1993 and has never been restored. Within the zone, there are no restrictions on capital movements, but there are few capital flows given the poor state of banking systems. The creation of a unified money market in WAEMU, an objective for a number of years, has in principle been achieved, but transactions are few. Most of the capital account transactions between residents of the zone and nonresidents are now subject only to a declaration for statistical purposes (December 1998 uniform exchange regulations).

The importance of trade among the countries of the two zones is limited (and, even more so, between them). Intra-WAEMU imports and exports are estimated to be about 12 percent of the region's total trade, while for CAEMC, the estimate is about 6 percent (Hugon, 1999). IMF *Direction of Trade Statistics* give lower figures (see Table 6.1 on page 20).

Currency union in the two zones was paralleled, to differing extents, by other institutions of regional integration. Before 1994, integration largely consisted of attempts at creating preferential trading areas. In West Africa, the West African Economic Community (WAEC) was founded in 1973, in response to the drawbacks of a predecessor customs union that attempted unsuccessfully to create a preferential internal regime in the absence of a common external tariff. WAEC created more adequate instruments of compensation for lost tariff revenues through a regional tax, the Taxe de Coopération Régionale. In 1994, WAEC was superseded by WAEMU, which established economic and monetary union, and has since put in place a common external tariff, introduced convergence criteria, and established a degree of surveillance over fiscal policies.

Regional integration has been slower in Central Africa. The Treaty creating CAEMC, signed in 1994, was finally ratified in June 1999. Although reforms pushed by its predecessor organization were in principle achieved (creating a common external tariff and a preferential internal tariff and the harmonization of indirect and business taxes), in fact they have been unevenly applied. Institutional development in CAEMC has not proceeded as fast as in WAEMU, although there are projects for enhancing intraregional surveillance in CAEMC too (Bank of France, 1999).

### The Common Monetary Area

The Common Monetary Area (CMA), or Rand Area, is composed of South Africa, Namibia, Lesotho, and Swaziland. The CMA is accompanied by a long-standing customs union, the Southern African Customs Union (SACU), with free circulation of goods internally and a common external tariff. Botswana left the CMA in 1976 but has remained a member of SACU. Labor mobility is relatively low between the smaller countries and South Africa (Tjirongo, 1998).

Each CMA country has its own currency, but given the size and degree of development of the three smaller members, the Reserve Bank of South Africa sets monetary policy. The three other countries' central banks function as currency boards, issuing their own currencies, but they are required to back their own currencies 100 percent with foreign assets. The South African rand circulates in each of the smaller countries (and is legal tender in Lesotho and Namibia).

The Reserve Bank of South Africa has generally avoided providing monetary financing and has achieved relatively low inflation. The rand floats against the major currencies and monetary policy is guided by an inflation target.

## Miscellaneous Asymmetric Monetary Unions

Examples of asymmetric monetary unions, whereby one country takes a leadership (hegemonic) role, are as follows:

- The Belgium-Luxembourg Economic Union (BLEU) has linked Belgium and Luxembourg since 1922. The countries issue separate currencies, exchangeable at par; Belgian currency is legal tender in Luxembourg but Luxembourg currency is not legal tender in Belgium. Currency union has been superseded since 1999 by the membership of both countries in a larger monetary union, the euro area. Monetary creation was controlled by the National Bank of Belgium, but Luxembourg had an input into decisions.
- The U.S. dollar is the medium of exchange in Panama, while the Panamanian currency (balboa) is a unit of account and exists only as silver coins. Panama has no influence over its monetary policy. While this has led to low interest rates (comparable to those in the United States), it also exposed Panama to freezing of U.S. accounts, leading to closure of Panama's banking system for two months in 1988, during the Noriega period (Moreno-Villalaz, 1999).

## Failed Currency Area: The Ruble Zone After the Demise of the Soviet Union

In the period prior to the break-up of the republics of the former Soviet Union and creation of the Commonwealth of Independent States (CIS) in 1991, separate republics had their own central banks. With the breakdown of central planning, control over the central banks' monetary expansion also broke down.

The ruble was an inconvertible currency whose internal convertibility was not even assured, making the ruble a poor medium of exchange. Incentives for excessive monetary expansion by each republic's central bank and lack of a centralized monetary policy led to uncontrolled inflation, making the ruble a poor store of value. Therefore, although the other CIS republics were heavily dependent on trade with Russia and not sufficiently advanced to create convertible currencies, they were led to introduce their own inconvertible currencies to be insulated from the monetary instability in Russia.

The other CIS republics, which were mainly oil importers, also faced different terms of trade shocks from Russia, an oil exporter, making separate currencies desirable (Gros, 1993).

## The East African Community

The East African Community (EAC) was formed by countries (Kenya, Tanganyika, and Uganda) that had a common currency, the East African shilling, under Britain's colonial rule.

In the 1960s, after independence, each country issued its own currency, but the EAC in 1967 specified free exchange between the national currencies at par.

After 1966, the rules of the currency board were loosened, giving governments more influence on their central banks and removing the floors on official reserves. Limits on advances to governments were undermined and credit was channeled to governments and public sector entities indirectly via the commercial banks (Guillaume and Stasavage, 2000).

In 1977, all three governments extended exchange controls to each other's currencies, effectively abolishing the monetary union (Cohen, 1998, p. 73).

# Appendix III    Comparative Performance of the CFA Franc Zone

There is now an extensive literature on whether the existence of a currency union in WAEMU and CAEMC has enhanced or hindered economic performance. A partial survey of this literature follows. Many studies have considered effects on intraregional trade, while others have examined broader aspects of economic performance, in particular growth and inflation. Some studies have quantified the effects of monetary union by doing a regression analysis on a cross-section of countries, including other structural determinants of performance, and tested for a significant difference in performance between members of monetary unions and nonmembers (e.g., by including a dummy variable for monetary union). Others have used a control group approach, looking at the average performance of CFA franc zone countries vis-à-vis a representative sample of comparable countries (e.g., other sub-Saharan African countries). In both cases, there is a potential problem of endogeneity; for instance, a third factor may explain why countries with better performance may also be members of monetary unions. Elbadawi and Majd (1996) correct for this endogeneity using a modified control group approach.

## Effects on Trade

The standard framework for considering the effect of membership in a monetary union on internal trade is the gravity model, which explains the extent of bilateral trade in either direction between a pair of countries by their respective size and per capita income (both affecting trade positively) and distance between them (negatively). Other variables can be included, such as whether the countries are contiguous, share a common language, have a common colonial past, or are part of a free trade area. In particular, we focus on the effect of a monetary union dummy variable.

Internal trade of the two CFA zones seems to be low—about 9 percent of their total trade for WAEMU countries and 3 percent of total trade for CAEMC countries—but low relative to what? The gravity model in fact predicts that their trade should be low, given levels of per capita income and total GDP. In contrast, the much higher income of EU countries exerts a strong "gravitational pull," which helps explain the large trade share of EU countries with the CFA zones. Consistent with this, trade among all pairs of sub-Saharan African countries tends to be low, whether members of monetary unions or not. Foroutan and Pritchett (1993) find that intra-African trade is no different from trade between other low- and middle-income developing countries. This conclusion is supported by Coe and Hoffmaister (1999), Rodrik (1999), and Subramanian and Tamirisa (2000).

Tests of the effects of membership in the CFA franc zones are mixed. Unfortunately, since the preferential trading arrangements overlap almost perfectly with the CFA zones, both sets of effects are captured. Foroutan and Pritchett (1993) find a significant positive effect on trade of the West African CFA zone, but not the Central African one. Elbadawi (1997) provides estimates for 1980–84 and 1986–90, finding that membership in the (then) West African Economic Community (WAEC) regional grouping[1] had a significant positive effect on internal trade in the first subperiod (increasing it by a factor of 32!), but a significant negative effect in the second (dividing it by 3). He concludes that effects are very much dependent on the interplay of the policy stance and membership in monetary union, as well as external factors (in particular, for the CFA franc zones, the fact that the French franc appreciated against the U.S. dollar in the second subperiod). As for the Central African CFA zone, membership did not seem to have a significant effect on trade for the countries concerned, consistent with the results of Foroutan and Pritchett.

Laporte (1998) also gets a significant and positive effect of WAMU membership on trade of the region. Moreover, the size of the effect increases over the three subperiods he considers (an elasticity of 3.49 in 1970–72, 3.90 in 1979–81, and 5.87 in 1989–91),

---
[1]The WAEC was superseded by WAEMU in 1994.

which he explains by strengthening economic cooperation accompanying the monetary union. Subramanian and Tamirisa (2000) also find a significant positive effect of CFA franc zone membership (both zones), using data for 1990, but the elasticity is estimated to be much smaller, only 1.68. For both studies, the dummy variable estimation does not permit distinguishing CFA franc zone membership from other forms of regional cooperation.

A larger set of countries could in principle distinguish between the two, since there are other monetary unions (e.g., the Eastern Caribbean Currency Union) that are not accompanied by preferential trading arrangements. Rose (2000) provides estimates of a gravity equation using all available United Nations data on 186 countries, dependencies, and territories; he includes dummy variables for both regional trade agreements and membership in a currency union. He concludes that the effect of the latter is significantly positive and robust, and membership in a monetary union multiplies bilateral trade of any two countries on average by a factor of three.

A different approach to quantifying effects on trade is provided by Guillaumont and Guillaumont-Jeanneney (1993), who look at the growth rate of bilateral trade relative to market growth for various groupings of countries (including CFA franc countries) and a control group of other developing countries. They find a significant effect of membership in the West African monetary union (and the associated trade arrangement) but none for the Central African monetary union. They suggest that the favorable effect on trade integration of monetary union is not automatic, but rather depends on the degree of solidarity of member countries.

## Effects on Output and Inflation

Studies on the wider effects of CFA franc membership underscore the very different performance of the zones in the years before and after 1985. Earlier studies (Guillaumont and Guillaumont, 1984; Devarajan and de Melo, 1987) had suggested that membership brought both higher growth and lower inflation. But Devarajan and de Melo (1992) highlighted the sharp difference between the 1986–90 period and earlier. They conclude that the later poor performance was due to inadequate policies in the face of negative terms of trade shocks and appreciation of their nominal (and real) effective exchange rates: "In principle, CFA Zone members have enough instruments with which to adjust their economies ... In practice they have been reluctant to use these other instruments." (p. 31). The conclusion that inflation performance was better for CFA zone members but growth was worse is robust to adjusting for endogeneity of regime choice (Elbadawi and Majd, 1996).

Another relevant study, by Hoffmaister, Roldós, and Wickham (1998), finds that terms of trade shocks have a greater influence on output in CFA countries, due to an exchange rate regime that does not buffer shocks.

# References

Allen, Polly Reynolds, 1976, "Organization and Administration of a Monetary Union," Princeton Studies in International Finance No. 38 (Princeton: Princeton University Press).

Asante, S.K.B., and Alex Ntim Abankwa, 1999, *A Study of the Impact of the West African Economic and Monetary Union (UEMOA) on Ghana,* draft report submitted to the Ministry of Finance, Accra, Ghana (June 15).

Azam, Jean-Paul, and Alpha Oumar Diakité, 1999, "Macroeconomic Policies and Exchange Rate Management in African Economies: The Guinean Case" (unpublished).

Bank of France, 1999, *La Zone Franc, Rapport 1998* (Paris: Bank of France).

Barro, Robert, and David Gordon, 1983, "Rules, Discretion and Reputation in a Model of Monetary Policy," *Journal of Monetary Economics*, Vol. 12 (July), pp. 101–21.

Cashin, Paul, and Catherine Pattillo, 2000, "Terms of Trade Shocks in Africa: Are They Short-Lived or Long-Lived?," IMF Working Paper 00/72 (Washington: International Monetary Fund).

Cobham, David, and Peter Robson, 1994, "Monetary Integration in Africa: A Deliberately European Perspective," *World Development*, Vol. 22 (No. 3), pp. 285–99.

Cohen, Benjamin J., 1998, *The Geography of Money* (Ithaca: Cornell University Press).

Coe, David, and Alexander Hoffmaister, 1999, "North-South Trade: Is Africa Unusual?," *Journal of African Economies*, Vol. 8 (No. 2), pp. 228–56.

Collier, Paul, 1991, "Africa's External Economic Relations, 1960–90," *African Affairs*, Vol. 90 (July), pp. 339–56.

———, and Jan Willem Gunning, 1999, "Why Has Africa Grown Slowly?," *Journal of Economic Perspectives,* Vol. 13 (No. 3), pp. 3–22.

Corden, W. M., 1972, "Monetary Integration," Essays in International Finance No. 93 (Princeton: Princeton University Press).

D'Almeida, Claude, 1998, *Le devenir du franc CFA* (Cotonou, Benin: Editions Perspectives Africaines, 2nd ed.).

Devarajan, Shantayanan, and Jaime de Melo, 1987, "Evaluating Participation in African Monetary Unions: A Statistical Analysis of the CFA Zones," *World Development*, Vol. 15 (No. 4), pp. 483–96.

———, 1992, "Membership in the CFA Zone: Odyssean Journey or Trojan Horse?," in *Economic Reform in Sub-Saharan Africa,* ed. by Ajay Chhibber and Stanley Fischer (Washington: World Bank).

Devarajan, Shantayanan, and Dani Rodrik, 1991, "Do the Benefits of Fixed Exchange Rates Outweigh Their Costs? The Franc Zone in Africa," NBER Working Paper No. 3727 (Cambridge, Massachusetts: National Bureau of Economic Research).

Easterly, William and Ross Levine, 1997, "Africa's Growth Tragedy: Policies and Ethnic Divisions," *Quarterly Journal of Economics,* Vol. 112 (November), pp. 1203–50.

Elbadawi, Ibrahim, 1997, "The Impact of Regional Trade and Monetary Schemes on Intra-Sub-Saharan Africa Trade," in *Regional Integration and Trade Liberalization in Sub-Saharan Africa, Vol. 3*, ed. by T. Ademola Oyejide, Ibrahim Elbadawi, and Paul Collier (New York: St. Martin's Press).

———, and Nader Majd, 1996, "Adjustment and Economic Performance Under a Fixed Exchange Rate: A Comparative Analysis of the CFA Zone," *World Development*, Vol. 24 (No. 5), pp. 939–51.

*Europa World Year Book of 1992*, Vols. I–II, 1992 (London: Europa Publications).

Foroutan, Faezeh, and Lant Pritchett, 1993, "Intra-Sub-Saharan African Trade: Is It Too Little?" *Journal of African Economies,* Vol. 2 (No. 5), pp. 74–105.

Frankel, Jeffrey, and Andrew Rose, 1998, "The Endogeneity of the Optimum Currency Area Criteria," *Economic Journal*, Vol. 108 (July), pp. 1009–25.

———, 2000, "Estimating the Effect of Currency Unions on Trade and Output," NBER Working Paper No. 7857 (Cambridge, Massachusetts: National Bureau of Economic Research).

Gnassou, A. Laure, 1999, "Après l'euro: quel statut juridique pour la zone franc africaine?" *Afrique contemporaine*, No. 189 (January–March), pp. 6–22.

Gros, Daniel, 1993, "Costs and Benefits of Economic and Monetary Union: An Application to the Former Soviet Union," in *Policy Issues in the Operation of Currency Unions,* ed. by P.R. Masson and M.P. Taylor (Cambridge, England: Cambridge University Press).

Guillaume, Dominique, and David Stasavage, 2000, "Improving Policy Credibility: Is There a Case for African Monetary Unions?" *World Development*, Vol. 28 (No. 8), pp. 1391–1407.

Guillaumont, Patrick, and Sylviane Guillaumont, 1984, *Zone franc et développement africain* (Paris: Economica).

# References

Guillaumont, Patrick, and Sylviane Guillaumont-Jeanneney, 1993, "L'Intégration économique: un nouvel enjeu pour la zone franc," *Revue d'économie du développement*, No. 2, pp. 83–112.

———, and Jean-François Brun, 1999, "How Instability Lowers African Growth," *Journal of African Economies*, Vol. 8 (No. 1), pp. 87–107.

Hanink, Dean, M., and J. Henry Owusu, 1998, "Has ECOWAS Promoted Trade Among Its Members," *Journal of African Economies*, Vol. 7 (No. 3), pp. 363–83.

Hausman, R., M. Gavin, C. Pages-Serra, and E. Stein, 1999, "Financial Turmoil and the Choice of Exchange Rate Regime" (unpublished; Washington: Inter-American Development Bank.

Hernández-Catá, Ernesto and others, 1998, *The West African Economic and Monetary Union: Recent Developments and Policy Issues*, IMF Occasional Paper No. 170 (Washington: International Monetary Fund).

Hoffmaister, Alexander, Jorge Roldós, and Peter Wickham, 1998, "Macroeconomic Fluctuations in Sub-Saharan Africa," *Staff Papers*, International Monetary Fund, Vol. 45 (January), pp. 132–60.

Hugon, Philippe, 1999, *La zone franc à l'heure de l'euro* (Paris: Karthala).

International Monetary Fund, 1999, *IMF Direction of Trade Statistics, 1999* (Washington).

———, 1999, *World Economic Outlook, October 1999*, World Economic and Financial Surveys (Washington).

———, 2000, "WAEMU: Recent Economic Developments and Regional Policy Issues in 1999," May (Washington).

Irving, Jacqueline, 1999, "For Better or for Worse: the Euro and the CFA Franc," *Africa Recovery*, Vol. 12 (April), pp. 1–29.

Kouyaté, Lansane, 2000, "ECOWAS Interim Report by the Executive Secretary," Abuja, Nigeria (April).

Laporte, Bertrand, 1998, "Contraintes Structurelles, Politiques Nationales et Cooperation Regionale: Determinants des Echanges entre les pays d'Afrique de l'Ouest?," *Canadian Journal of Development Studies*, Vol. 19 (No. 1), pp. 97–116.

Mainwaring, Scott, and Matthew Soberg Shugart, eds., 1997, *Presidentialism and Democracy in Latin America* (Cambridge, England: Cambridge University Press).

Mamdou, Ousmande Samba, 1997, "The CFAF Devaluation, Naira Parallel Exchange Rate and Niger's Competitiveness," *Journal of African Economies*, Vol. 6 (March), pp. 85–111.

Masson, Paul, Miguel Savastano, and Sunil Sharma, 1997, "The Scope for Inflation Targeting in Developing Countries," IMF Working Paper 97/130 (Washington: International Monetary Fund).

McPherson, Malcolm F., and Steven Radelet, 1991, "Economic Reform in the Gambia: Policies, Politics, Foreign Aid, and Luck," in *Reforming Economic Systems in Developing Countries*, ed. by Dwight Perkins and Michael Roemer (Cambridge, Massachusetts: Harvard University Press).

Monga, Célestin, and Jean-Claude Tchatchouang, 1996, *Sortir du Piège Monétaire* (Paris: Economica).

Moreno-Villalaz, Juan Luis, 1999, "Lessons from the Monetary Experience of Panama: A Dollar Economy with Financial Integration," *Cato Journal*, Vol. 18 (Winter), pp. 421–39.

Morris, Stephen, 1995, "Inflation Dynamics and the Parallel Market for Foreign Exchange," *Journal of Development Economics*, Vol. 46 (April), pp. 295-316.

Moser, Gary, Scott Rogers, Reinhold van Til, and others, 1997, *Nigeria: Experience with Structural Adjustment*, IMF Occasional Paper No. 148 (Washington: International Monetary Fund).

Mundell, Robert, 1961, "A Theory of Optimum Currency Areas," *American Economic Review*, Vol. 51 (September), pp. 657–65.

Nascimento, Jean-Claude, 1994, "Monetary Policy in Unified Currency Areas: The Cases of the CAMA and ECCA during 1976–90," IMF Working Paper 94/11 (Washington: International Monetary Fund).

Organization for Economic Cooperation and Development, 1972, *Stock of Private Direct Investments by D.A.C. Countries in Developing Countries, End 1967* (Paris: OECD).

Pinto, Brian, 1989, "Black Market Premia, Exchange Rate Unification, and Inflation in Sub-Saharan Africa, *World Bank Economic Review*, Vol. 3, pp. 321–38.

———, 1991, "Black Markets for Foreign Exchange, Real Exchange Rates and Inflation, *Journal of International Economics*, Vol. 30 (February), pp. 121–35.

Radelet, Steven, C., 1993, "Gambia's Economic Recovery: Policy Reforms, Foreign Aid, or Rain?" *Journal of Policy Modeling*, Vol. 15 (June), pp. 251–76.

Randall, Ruby, 1998, "Interest Rate Spreads in the Eastern Caribbean," IMF Working Paper 98/59 (Washington: International Monetary Fund).

Rodrik, Dani, 1999, *The New Global Economy and Developing Countries: Making Openness Work* (Washington: Overseas Development Council).

Rose, Andrew, 2000, "One Money, One Market: Estimating the Effect of Common Currencies on Trade," NBER Working Paper No. 7432 (Cambridge, Massachusetts: National Bureau of Economic Research).

Sala-i-Martin, Xavier, and Jeffrey Sachs, 1992, "Fiscal Federalism and Optimum Currency Areas: Evidence for Europe from the United States," in *Establishing a Central Bank: Issues in Europe and Lessons from the U.S.*, ed. by M.B. Canzoneri, V. Grilli, and P.R. Masson (Cambridge, England: Cambridge University Press).

Stasavage, David, 1996, "The CFA Franc Zone and Fiscal Discipline," *Journal of African Economies*, Vol. 6 (No. 1), pp. 132–67.

Subramanian, Arvind, and Natalia Tamirisa, 2000, "Africa. An Overtrader" (unpublished; Washington: International Monetary Fund).

Tavlas, George, 2000, "On the Exchange Rate as a Nominal Anchor: The Rise and Fall of the Credibility Hypothesis," *The Economic Record*, Vol. 76 (June), pp. 183–201.

Tjirongo, Meshack Tunee, 1998, "Exchange Rate Policy Options for Namibia" (Ph.D. dissertation; Oxford, England: University of Oxford).

Tornell, Aaron, and Andrés Velasco, 1995, "Fixed versus Flexible Exchange Rates: Which Provides More Fis-

# REFERENCES

cal Discipline?" NBER Working Paper No. 5108 (Cambridge, Massachusetts: National Bureau of Economic Research).

United Nations Conference on Trade and Development, 1999, *World Investment Report—1999 Foreign Direct Investment and the Challenge of Development* (New York: United Nations).

Van Beek, Frits, and others, 2000, *The Eastern Caribbean Currency Union: Institutions, Performance, and Policy Issues,* IMF Occasional Paper No. 195 (Washington: International Monetary Fund).

World Bank, 2000, "Part II: West Africa, Key Trends and Regional Perspectives," West Africa Regional Assistance Strategy Discussion Paper (unpublished).

Yeats, Alexander, 1998, "What Can Be Expected from African Regional Trade Arrangements? Some Empirical Evidence," Policy Research Working Paper No. 2004 (Washington: World Bank).

## Recent Occasional Papers of the International Monetary Fund

204. Monetary Union in West Africa (ECOWAS): Is It Desirable and How Could It Be Achieved? by Paul Masson and Catherine Pattillo. 2001.

203. Modern Banking and OTC Derivatives Markets: The Transformation of Global Finance and Its Implications for Systemic Risk, by Garry J. Schinasi, R. Sean Craig, Burkhard Drees, and Charles Kramer. 2000.

202. Adopting Inflation Targeting: Practical Issues for Emerging Market Countries, by Andrea Schaechter, Mark R. Stone, and Mark Zelmer. 2000.

201. Developments and Challenges in the Caribbean Region, by Samuel Itam, Simon Cueva, Erik Lundback, Janet Stotsky, and Stephen Tokarick. 2000.

200. Pension Reform in the Baltics: Issues and Prospects, by Jerald Schiff, Niko Hobdari, Axel Schimmelpfennig, and Roman Zytek. 2000.

199. Ghana: Economic Development in a Democratic Environment, by Sérgio Pereira Leite, Anthony Pellechio, Luisa Zanforlin, Girma Begashaw, Stefania Fabrizio, and Joachim Harnack. 2000.

198. Setting Up Treasuries in the Baltics, Russia, and Other Countries of the Former Soviet Union: An Assessment of IMF Technical Assistance, by Barry H. Potter and Jack Diamond. 2000.

197. Deposit Insurance: Actual and Good Practices, by Gillian G.H. Garcia. 2000.

196. Trade and Trade Policies in Eastern and Southern Africa, by a staff team led by Arvind Subramanian, with Enrique Gelbard, Richard Harmsen, Katrin Elborgh-Woytek, and Piroska Nagy. 2000.

195. The Eastern Caribbean Currency Union—Institutions, Performance, and Policy Issues, by Frits van Beek, José Roberto Rosales, Mayra Zermeño, Ruby Randall, and Jorge Shepherd. 2000.

194. Fiscal and Macroeconomic Impact of Privatization, by Jeffrey Davis, Rolando Ossowski, Thomas Richardson, and Steven Barnett. 2000.

193. Exchange Rate Regimes in an Increasingly Integrated World Economy, by Michael Mussa, Paul Masson, Alexander Swoboda, Esteban Jadresic, Paolo Mauro, and Andy Berg. 2000.

192. Macroprudential Indicators of Financial System Soundness, by a staff team led by Owen Evans, Alfredo M. Leone, Mahinder Gill, and Paul Hilbers. 2000.

191. Social Issues in IMF-Supported Programs, by Sanjeev Gupta, Louis Dicks-Mireaux, Ritha Khemani, Calvin McDonald, and Marijn Verhoeven. 2000.

190. Capital Controls: Country Experiences with Their Use and Liberalization, by Akira Ariyoshi, Karl Habermeier, Bernard Laurens, Inci Ötker-Robe, Jorge Iván Canales Kriljenko, and Andrei Kirilenko. 2000.

189. Current Account and External Sustainability in the Baltics, Russia, and Other Countries of the Former Soviet Union, by Donal McGettigan. 2000.

188. Financial Sector Crisis and Restructuring: Lessons from Asia, by Carl-Johan Lindgren, Tomás J.T. Balino, Charles Enoch, Anne-Marie Gulde, Marc Quintyn, and Leslie Teo. 1999.

187. Philippines: Toward Sustainable and Rapid Growth, Recent Developments and the Agenda Ahead, by Markus Rodlauer, Prakash Loungani, Vivek Arora, Charalambos Christofides, Enrique G. De la Piedra, Piyabha Kongsamut, Kristina Kostial, Victoria Summers, and Athanasios Vamvakidis. 2000.

186. Anticipating Balance of Payments Crises: The Role of Early Warning Systems, by Andrew Berg, Eduardo Borensztein, Gian Maria Milesi-Ferretti, and Catherine Pattillo. 1999.

185. Oman Beyond the Oil Horizon: Policies Toward Sustainable Growth, edited by Ahsan Mansur and Volker Treichel. 1999.

184. Growth Experience in Transition Countries, 1990–98, by Oleh Havrylyshyn, Thomas Wolf, Julian Berengaut, Marta Castello-Branco, Ron van Rooden, and Valerie Mercer-Blackman. 1999.

183. Economic Reforms in Kazakhstan, Kyrgyz Republic, Tajikistan, Turkmenistan, and Uzbekistan, by Emine Gürgen, Harry Snoek, Jon Craig, Jimmy McHugh, Ivailo Izvorski, and Ron van Rooden. 1999.

182. Tax Reform in the Baltics, Russia, and Other Countries of the Former Soviet Union, by a staff team led by Liam Ebrill and Oleh Havrylyshyn. 1999.

## OCCASIONAL PAPERS

181. The Netherlands: Transforming a Market Economy, by C. Maxwell Watson, Bas B. Bakker, Jan Kees Martijn, and Ioannis Halikias. 1999.
180. Revenue Implications of Trade Liberalization, by Liam Ebrill, Janet Stotsky, and Reint Gropp. 1999.
179. Disinflation in Transition: 1993–97, by Carlo Cottarelli and Peter Doyle. 1999.
178. IMF-Supported Programs in Indonesia, Korea, and Thailand: A Preliminary Assessment, by Timothy Lane, Atish Ghosh, Javier Hamann, Steven Phillips, Marianne Schulze-Ghattas, and Tsidi Tsikata. 1999.
177. Perspectives on Regional Unemployment in Europe, by Paolo Mauro, Eswar Prasad, and Antonio Spilimbergo. 1999.
176. Back to the Future: Postwar Reconstruction and Stabilization in Lebanon, edited by Sena Eken and Thomas Helbling. 1999.
175. Macroeconomic Developments in the Baltics, Russia, and Other Countries of the Former Soviet Union, 1992–97, by Luis M. Valdivieso. 1998.
174. Impact of EMU on Selected Non–European Union Countries, by R. Feldman, K. Nashashibi, R. Nord, P. Allum, D. Desruelle, K. Enders, R. Kahn, and H. Temprano-Arroyo. 1998.
173. The Baltic Countries: From Economic Stabilization to EU Accession, by Julian Berengaut, Augusto Lopez-Claros, Françoise Le Gall, Dennis Jones, Richard Stern, Ann-Margret Westin, Effie Psalida, Pietro Garibaldi. 1998.
172. Capital Account Liberalization: Theoretical and Practical Aspects, by a staff team led by Barry Eichengreen and Michael Mussa, with Giovanni Dell'Ariccia, Enrica Detragiache, Gian Maria Milesi-Ferretti, and Andrew Tweedie. 1998.
171. Monetary Policy in Dollarized Economies, by Tomás Baliño, Adam Bennett, and Eduardo Borensztein. 1998.
170. The West African Economic and Monetary Union: Recent Developments and Policy Issues, by a staff team led by Ernesto Hernández-Catá and comprising Christian A. François, Paul Masson, Pascal Bouvier, Patrick Peroz, Dominique Desruelle, and Athanasios Vamvakidis. 1998.
169. Financial Sector Development in Sub-Saharan African Countries, by Hassanali Mehran, Piero Ugolini, Jean Phillipe Briffaux, George Iden, Tonny Lybek, Stephen Swaray, and Peter Hayward. 1998.
168. Exit Strategies: Policy Options for Countries Seeking Greater Exchange Rate Flexibility, by a staff team led by Barry Eichengreen and Paul Masson with Hugh Bredenkamp, Barry Johnston, Javier Hamann, Esteban Jadresic, and Inci Ötker. 1998.
167. Exchange Rate Assessment: Extensions of the Macroeconomic Balance Approach, edited by Peter Isard and Hamid Faruqee. 1998
166. Hedge Funds and Financial Market Dynamics, by a staff team led by Barry Eichengreen and Donald Mathieson with Bankim Chadha, Anne Jansen, Laura Kodres, and Sunil Sharma. 1998.
165. Algeria: Stabilization and Transition to the Market, by Karim Nashashibi, Patricia Alonso-Gamo, Stefania Bazzoni, Alain Féler, Nicole Laframboise, and Sebastian Paris Horvitz. 1998.
164. MULTIMOD Mark III: The Core Dynamic and Steady-State Model, by Douglas Laxton, Peter Isard, Hamid Faruqee, Eswar Prasad, and Bart Turtelboom. 1998.
163. Egypt: Beyond Stabilization, Toward a Dynamic Market Economy, by a staff team led by Howard Handy. 1998.
162. Fiscal Policy Rules, by George Kopits and Steven Symansky. 1998.
161. The Nordic Banking Crises: Pitfalls in Financial Liberalization? by Burkhard Drees and Ceyla Pazarbaşıoğlu. 1998.
160. Fiscal Reform in Low-Income Countries: Experience Under IMF-Supported Programs, by a staff team led by George T. Abed and comprising Liam Ebrill, Sanjeev Gupta, Benedict Clements, Ronald McMorran, Anthony Pellechio, Jerald Schiff, and Marijn Verhoeven. 1998.

**Note:** For information on the title and availability of Occasional Papers not listed, please consult the IMF Publications Catalog or contact IMF Publication Services.